SOCIETY IS THE AUTHORITY

LAW AND THE RUSSELL PRIDGEON CASE

Mary W Maxwell, LLB

ISBN 979-8-89121-265-7

Keywords:
accountability in legal profession, judicial offenses, gag orders, Russell Pridgeon, Patrick O'Dea, MK-Ultra, child sexual abuse, Family Law Act, child trafficking, Rachel Vaughan, Philip Allott, mutiny, Kevin Annett, lexmen, Association Papers

Author:

Mary W Maxwell, PhD, LLB
175 Loudon Rd, Apt 6,
Concord NH 03301 USA

Email address: MaxwellMaryLLB@gmail.com

Author's websites:

ConstitutionAndTruth.com
JaharCompletelyInnocent.com

Cover photo by Anita Rajcany

To Diane DeVere, connector of dots,
who immigrated
to Australia in 1948

and to the memory of my wonderful husband,
George Maxwell,
who immigrated to Australia in 1959

PREFACE

As the world knows, Australia fell from its place of esteem during the Covid years. The state of Victoria was especially tyrannical under "Dictator Dan." The state of Western Australia passed legislation to allow forcible removal of underwear (you can't make this stuff up) in aid of forcible vaccination. South Australia continued its regime of ignoring the murderers of children.

In October 2018, two men in New South Wales were falsely arrested for "child-stealing," in order to cover up the fact that it was officials of the government who were really behind this crime. The two men have been diddled with for years, awaiting "trial."

By April 2023, one of them -- Russell Pridgeon, a physician -- had had enough and wrote a book about child stealing, entitled "Everybody Knows." That turned Australia around. Russell's friends, who wish to stay out of the limelight, had given him the downlow on the mechanisms of corruption in the legal system. Once enough Aussies saw it, the house of cards began to fall.

The trial of Russell Pridgeon and Patrick O'Dea was scheduled to begin 22 May 2023. Trying to stir up some righteousness (or was it vengeance?), I defended them in several articles. Dee McLachlan provided the venue at her website GumshoeNews.com. Now they are collected in this book. Please enjoy and share them.

I hope this book stimulates some tourism to beautiful continent Australia ("Oz" to locals). You can hardly imagine a better place. The book's theme is that we have already conquered the reign of the amoral, or immoral, powerful bastards. (I'm a dual citizen of US and Oz.) Yes, I consider it guaranteed.

If you are a lawyer, start by reading Chapter 5, and please blush.

Mary W Maxwell   Concord New Hampshire   26 June 2023

TABLE OF CONTENTS

Part Four: Kafka

Part Five: Evils

Part Six: Future

FOREWORD, from Judith

Then was the kingdom of Nabuchodonosor exalted, and his heart was elevated: and he sent to all that dwelt in Cilicia and Damascus … and beyond the river Jordan even to Jerusalem, and all the land of Jesse till you come to the borders of Ethiopia.

Then king Nabuchodonosor being angry and swore by his throne that he would revenge himself of all those countries. His thoughts were to bring all the earth under his empire. He called Holofernes the general of his armies. And said: Go out against all the kingdoms, and bring [them] under my yoke.

Holofernes called the captains and officers and he mustered men, a hundred and twenty thousand. And he passed over the Euphrates and he forced all the stately cities that were there. All that resisted him he slew, and he set all the corn on fire, and he caused all the trees and vineyards to be cut down.

Achior said to Holofernes: When the king of Egypt oppressed the Hebrews, and made slaves of them to labour in clay and brick, in the building of his cities, they cried to their Lord, and he struck the whole land of Egypt with divers plagues. Holofernes being in a violent passion, said to Achior: …. Set guards at the springs that they may not draw water out of them. And he placed all round about a hundred men at every spring.

Now Judith a widow had [overheard]. And she was exceedingly beautiful. And she was greatly renowned among all, because she feared the Lord very much, neither was there anyone that spoke an ill word of her. And Judith, falling down prostrate before the Lord, cried Give me fortitude that I may overthrow him.

And she washed her body, and anointed herself with ointment, and plaited her hair. And the Lord also gave her more beauty, so that she appeared to all men's eyes incomparably lovely. And she gave to her maid a bottle of wine to carry, and a vessel of oil, and dry figs, and bread and cheese, and went out. The watchmen of the Assyrians met her and stopped her, saying: whither goest thou? she answered: I am a daughter of the Hebrews, and I am fled from them, as I knew they would be made a prey to you. And they brought her to the tent of Holofernes, telling him of her.

And when she was come into his presence, Holofernes was sitting under a canopy, which was woven with emeralds and precious stones. She bowed down to him. Then Holofernes said to her: Be of good comfort, and fear not. But tell me, why it hath pleased thee to come to us? And Judith said: For the industry of thy mind is spoken of among all nations. For drought of water the Hebrews will be among the dead. Knowing this, I fled from them.

And it came to pass on the fourth day, that Holofernes made a supper for his servants, and said to Vagao his eunuch: go, and persuade that Hebrew woman, to consent of her own accord to dwell with me. And the heart of Holofernes was smitten, for he was burning with the desire of her. And Holofernes drank exceeding much wine, so much as he had never drunk in his life.

Judith was alone in the chamber. But Holofernes lay on his bed, fast asleep, being exceedingly drunk. And she went to the pillar that was at his bed's head, and loosed his sword that hung tied upon it. And when she had drawn it out, she took him by the hair of his head, and said: Strengthen me, O Lord God, at this hour. And she struck twice upon his neck, and cut off his head.

And after a while she went out, and delivered the head of Holofernes to her maid, and bade her put it into her sack. And Judith from afar cried to the watchmen upon the walls: Open the gates for God is with us. Then she brought forth the head of Holofernes out of the sack, and shewed it the Hebrews, saying: Behold the head of the general of the army of the Assyrians. Give all of you glory to God, because he is good, because his mercy endureth for ever. And all the people said: So be it, so be it.

In a chamber, Vagao stood before the curtain. But when he perceived no motion, he came near to the curtain, and lifting it up, and seeing the body of Holofernes, lying upon the ground, without the head, he cried out, with weeping, and rent his garments.

Table of Authorities -- Laws and Cases Cited in This Book

Australian Commonwealth [Cth] Law:

State Laws: ***Queensland, New South Wales, South Australia:***

Court Rulings in Australia:

Other Law References:

American Authoritative Documents, Statutes and Cases

US Supreme Court Rulings:

US District or Appellate Court Cases:

Other Jurisdictions Mentioned:

Part One: Breakthrough 1. We are saved! WE ARE SAVED!

From Dee McLachlan's cover for Pridgeon's book Everybody Knows

I always knew it. Maybe you didn't know? Maybe pessimism was the order of the day for you? But I knew it. Without a single doubt! I knew, pardon the simplicity of this, that good would win out over bad. Heroes would arise. Spring would come again.

I know that from biology, but we won't go into that explanation right now. Let's just look at the happy facts for Australia in this wondrous year, Twenty-Twenty-Three.

For the last decade, since 2013, our dear website, Gumshoe-News.com, has chronicled the abysmal fall of Australia. It fell and fell — no point denying it. Downaroonie was the only direction. We spent time analyzing the trends. We identified some of the miscreants (don't you love that word?).

Ah, wait, I just asked Google for "miscreant," and was provided with these synonyms: perverse, reprehensible, unprincipled, vicious, wicked. Plus, MacmillanDictionary.com threw in: skullduggery, hank-panky, jiggery-pokery, and slickness.

Slickness? I am about to tell, you, Ladies and Gentlemen, that certain miscreants did not have enough slickness to carry out their evil mission. And their jiggery-pokery was their undoing. I give them credit for jigging and poking "to the best of their ability" — but it was bound to fail.

You see, folks, there are standards. Yep, standards in the human heart. People do not like a mess. Even a 3-year-old can sense meanness in a relationship and knows it doesn't belong there. Not that a 3-year-old can make it go right. A fifty-three-year-old can't do it either, if millions around him are participating in the mess, and surrendering to the meanness.

Gumshoe has chronicled how the continent under the Southern Cross went into a hellish state. To name just one name, Rachel Vaughan showed, from the experience of her truly wicked father, that people had declined to the point of torturing, traumatizing, and even eating one another. Madness!

Rachel did her duty, exposing the apparent vice-grip on a whole police department. But she couldn't break the system.

So who now has broken it? The miscreants themselves broke it. Hooray! What dumbies! Wait till you read Russell Pridgeon's book *Everybody Knows*. He has acted heroically. But history was just waiting for him to come along. The various circumstances added up and then: Pow. Bang. Wham. Crash.

It's a beautiful book. Time after time the authorities broke the law — on the record! They have been so used to arrogant self-confidence, and so cushioned by impunity from the public, that they just kept putting their foot in it. Meanwhile, Russell Pridgeon carefully recorded every wrong legal move.

While reading it, the thought that came floating into my head was "Dr Pridgeon is a soft-spoken man, but he is carrying a stainless-steel cricket bat." It is actually the *Everybody Knows* book that is his stainless-steel cricket bat. You sure wouldn't want to be members of government trying to imprison him and his co-hero Patrick O'Dea at their trial, would you?

By the way, here is a lovely snippet from the book. Russell is speaking of Patrick "a man of noted courage through his life." Here I'll refer to the occasion on which Operation Noetic cracked down on Patrick -- and on Russell whom they had the creativity to call a Kingpin of child trafficking. Yes, a kingpin, no less!

Media were in full attendance at the arrest. Says the author of *Everybody Knows*:

"After we were arrested and our property was searched and seized, we were taken to the cells at the Grafton Police Station. I found the attending Grafton Police to be courteous and kind, as they have been during the daily Bail Reporting that I was forced to do by my Bail Conditions in the years since then. [Fathom it — having to report seven days a week— fathom it!]

Ordinary Police are decent people, they do a job that is difficult and demanding. They share the loathing of child abuse that is felt by ordinary decent Australians. As a rural GP, I was made aware of the arduous and demoralising working conditions that rural Police endured. I could only admire them.

"The next day I was driven by Australian Federal Police from Grafton to Brisbane, where Patrick and I were imprisoned for the next 3 days. …The wonderful thing about having been a national serviceman in the Rhodesian Army was how perfectly it prepared us for life in prison. I watched Patrick and saw him slip into the same routines we knew so well in the army: contending with unpleasantness from aggressive thugs by standing quietly at ease, with feet apart, arms behind us, hands together, looking straight ahead into the middle distance, with an expressionless face. We had been shat on by experts, these people were only amateurs."

"After the charges have been laid, Patrick and I were separated because of our Bail conditions. These specified that I was not allowed to 'contact, threaten, intimidate or harass, directly or indirectly' 42 people, most of whom I did not know, or had never heard of.

"So we were silenced and isolated, the same techniques that are used on the child victims of abuse, and for the same reasons. If the Australian public became aware of the abuse, and the misfeasance that concealed and enabled the ongoing abuse, they would be horrified, and very angry."

Blurbs on back cover of US edition of *Everybody Knows*

Unless the Prosecution empanel a hand-picked and corrupt jury, they can never get a conviction. -- *Graeme Bell, NSW.*

We'd better realize that official deceptions and unlawfulness are corroding society. The key thing is for Aussies is to say goodbye to fear, and cultivate solidarity. Let Operation Noetic teach the police a lesson. Cops have told us that they hate to grab kids from their homes. And let judges see the light! -- *Dee McLachlan, VIC.*

Binni's Foreword says it all: An adult protector was what she longed for. She dreamed of a Russell Pridgeon but none showed up. Why are we punishing the real Russell Pridgeon? The world should thank him for bringing this out into the open. And we deeply thank the kids, too. -- *Michelle Roderick, mortician (ret) Florida.*

The tragic irony regarding the plight of Dr Russell Pridgeon and Patrick O'Dea is they left Mugabe's autocratic Zimbabwe in search of a country where they would be free, their fundamental human rights, protected. This was a mistake; they both rue the day they decided on Australia. -- *Hannes Wessels, Rhodesian born writer and conservationist.*

Everybody knows! French poet Charles Peguy wrote: "He who does not bellow the truth when he knows the truth makes himself the accomplice of liars and forgers." -- *Diane DeVere, Geelong VIC, historian of Tavistock and a leading figure in Indigenous education.*

Russell: "We had been shat on by experts [in the Rhodesian army]; these people [the pedo-protectors] were only amateurs." Amateurs they may be, but vicious criminals they all are. Not only to the helpers of the children, but also towards the children. -- *Mal Hughes, Perth, Vietnam vet, author of A History of Kwinana.*

'Suppression order,' my arse. The authorities and the media have now entrapped themselves. Yay! And did the AFP really 'capture' Pridgeon? Oh, come on. *Mary Maxwell, LLB (late of Adelaide).*

I am totally exhilarated by Russell's book. Not because of its fight against child abuse — which is what drives Russell — but because of the way it shows the contemporary hopelessness of our courts (US and Australia). Which is what drives me.

So, my book here is mostly about law. Russell has given us the key. He has spotlighted the gap between what good law offers and how it is flagrantly twisted by persons in "authority." But he doesn't stop there. He marches out and arrests them. I mean he specifies what each bad cop or bad judge has done -- done to him! But it doesn't sound like whingeing. It's liberating. We *need* this.

My field is sociobiology -- natural man. Our emotions and our rationality are tied to a distant past. We did not evolve to live in groups of millions. We can't change our brain now, but it is normal and historically commonplace -- ordinary, run-of-the-mill -- for us to talk about and ponder new directions for our way of life.

Why do I say the Pridgeon book is a turning point? Partly it is because Russell takes a school-masterly approach, and can back it up with manliness. He and his buddy -- i.e., partner in "crime" -- Patrick O'Dea went about the business of helping children (for him it was 2 girls; for Patrick it was one boy) who got pulled away from their Mum. Arrayed against them were the AFP, Australian Federal Police, the who arrested them under "Operation Noetic."

Give me a chance to show you the score. Here in Part One, I outline the racket of child trafficking. Chapter 5 is the nub and I mean the nub. It is a fantastic ruling by a judge trained in the art of using words to completely change the essence of the reality.

The other Parts are on **Law** -- be still my fluttering heart -- and then on **Africa** (a bit of bio on the Boys from Bulaweyo, meant to make you think of where our excellent immigrants come from, and to provide some comic relief -- in particular go to Chapter 11 go there when you are feeling low). Then parts on **Kafka**, so to speak, and **Evils** -- I used to avoid the word *evil* but now it's unavoidable -- and **Future**, our fun, fun future.
Please join me.

2. How a Judge Can Destroy a Mother's Life

Mona Gudbranson, a grandmother, gives sad Congressional Testimony, via Bill Windsor's Lawless America series, on YouTube.com, in 2013

Dear Person who cares about the law, I am trying to help a very worthy doctor who is being subjected to an utterly bogus criminal trial, that will start someday in 2023 in Brisbane District Court. I fear he will "bogusly" be found guilty. Why? Because judges are no longer judges. They work for a higher power. Maybe not all of them, but why aren't the good ones criticizing this practice?

In 2017, Australia finished its Royal Commission on child sexual abuse, in which 8,000 victims were interviewed. Prime Minister Scott Morrison offered a formal apology for the government's lack of caring. So, no one can say abuse does not occur. Yet when a mother today makes a call to a hotline to say that her 'ex' has abused her children, she is by no means offered any help!

Perhaps the average citizen thinks the hotline would cause the police to check out the man's behavior. Certainly you'd think the kid would be given protection. But no. There is a standard procedure in place. The man does NOT get investigated. The child does NOT get protected. And, irony of ironies, the mother ends up in legal trouble.

This chapter will show you exactly what happens in Oz (Australia) and what a mother typically will go through. But it is mirrored in other countries. I allege that the judges are the ones most responsible for it and that it is blatantly a criminal enterprise.

These five-stages can be called Kid Kidnap or the KK system:
1. The mother will immediately be treated as a mental case. On the very day she reports the abuse of her child, she may be pressured to go to a local hospital for a psychological exam. Wait, didn't I just say that a Royal Commission already established that child abuse is rife? Then why not make it an initial presumption that Mum is telling the truth?

2. Next, the kid may be taken away. What? A suffering child -- or any child -- needs its Mum. It's very well known that a sudden separation is traumatic, causing lifelong damage. But no judge shows any recognition of this fact. It's as though all of normalcy has disappeared -- they live in a different world.

3. And what is Dad's next move? It is so unlike what you'd expect a pedophile to do, that I have to believe someone has taught him this cute trick. He fronts up at Family Court to request custody of the child. Yes, he does. Amazing. He should be hiding from police, not striding into a courthouse, right?

4. The upshot of Dad's doing that, is fourfold: (a) a long career of court activity now begins, for the mother. All her money will disappear into legal fees, and for years her time will go into preparing for the next hearing, (b) in court, she will constantly face the accusation that she has "alienated" the child from its father and that, in order to do that, she coached the child to lie about sexual abuse!

(c) any further attempt by her to get help from the police will be met by their saying solemnly that they cannot get involved whilst a case is before the courts. "The matter is sub judice." (d) the kid may have told a "mandatory reporter," such as a teacher; a doctor or may have provided evidence of injury. But the teachers' reports will be down-graded, and the medical evidence will be "lost."

5. At this point, or sooner, Child Protection Services -- the dreaded CPS -- will get into Mother's life. Why? To prevent her from "doing emotional harm to the child," Imagine such an insult! Mum will have to ask for "access visits."

Thus, once a week, she has the privilege of watching her child grow up, for an hour or two, while a social worker sits there and prevents any talk about Dad and also prevents the mum from giving gifts. Most likely the kid will be partly taken in by the buzz about mum not being quite OK anymore.

Those are the five standard features that thousands of mums have been through. As far as I'm aware, it never ends happily. Ask: Does someone have to whisper to the judge, as he's donning his robe, "Remember now, don't show any respect to the woman. Never refer to the child's needs. Exhibit total skepticism about the reported abuse." If so, who is the whisperer? I don't know.

Incidentally, many judges are male -- but female judges act the same way. Note: when I say "mum," I really mean "the protective parent", as sometimes the shoe is on the other foot: it's the mum who does the sexual abuse, or is renting her kid out for prostitution. If the dad calls the police, he, too, will get the KK treatment.

The Case of Dr Russell Pridgeon

When the law becomes hopeless, you have to try to get around the law. In Adelaide we had a wonderful professor of Child Development, the late Freda Briggs. She was aware of KK. In 2014 she encouraged a person, Dr Pridgeon, to help a mother escape. It's morally right to do so, and it is legal. For example, the **Queensland Criminal Code sec 286 makes it a crime NOT to protect** a child from harm. That said, there are other laws that tell you not to breach any court order. So, if the Family Law judge has said "X" gets custody, and you snatch the kid from X's custody, you are **committing a crime of breaking a court order.**

Pridgeon did help a mum with two daughters. She had illegally grabbed them. He drove them in his car to safety, set her up with the kids in a unit, and paid their rent. That was in 2014 and since then, for 9 years, he's had to be worried about his law-breaking. In 2015, that mum got arrested for stealing her own children. Did the cops hand two girls back to their abuser? Yes. It's *de rigueur.* So they've been with Dad for the last 8 years and the mum has hardly seen them. She was arrested and has been awaiting her trial.

Operation Noetic Arrests Pridgeon, O'Dea, and Others

I met Dr Russell Pridgeon in Queensland in 2019. He was wearing a leg tracker and had to sit near a charger for 2 hours each day. That was one of a dozen inconveniences he was subjected to. Another pain, that we all can relate to, was the taking of his computer by the police. He has never been able to get it back. Of course this is harassment. Police have no need to keep it. If it's his emails they're after, they need only ask Big Brother for a copy.

In October 2018, Pridgeon and Patrick O'Dea had been "netted" in a federal police operation. MSM (mainstream media, such as Brisbane's *Courier Times*) gave it the full drama treatment. They reported that Russell was a Kingpin (no less) in a child abduction racket. It was also referred to as a 'syndicate' and that cops had worked hard for two years to find it. What utter nonsense!

In May 2018, Russell had informed the Commonwealth Director of Public Prosecutions of what he was doing. He had pleaded for the CDPP and Minister for Child Safety Di Farmer to help rescue the kids. They gave him the cold shoulder. I say **they are gangsters**. Yep. They may all be dressed properly as law enforcement but that's deceiving. Actions speak louder than badges.

They stacked charges against Pridgeon; 5 were later dropped, including the eye-catching one that he "dealt in the proceeds of crime." A month after the dramatic 2018 arrest, the Medical Council cancelled Pridgeon's medical license. They are not allowed to do this; only a conviction, not an indictment, can be used. Three years later he got his license back, when the New South Wales Supreme Court, Court of Appeal, fortunately, wrote:

> "It could not (yet) be said that Dr Pridgeon's alleged defiance of the court's orders undermines the rule of law ... [his] guilt is not a foregone conclusion."

The government is heavily invested in blaming citizens to cover their own guilt for child trafficking. The government deploys its expertise in lying, intimidating, and weaponizing the law for this. Russell is now charged only with 'perverting the course of justice.'

3. Magistrate Gets Vaporized by His Own Efforts

-- *A gumshoe-DM adaption*

You may remember our friend Serene Teffaha who was busy gathering up a large number of Australian citizens to form a class action against the 2021 Lockdown. Seems reasonable enough. You could even imagine that hundreds of lawyers might imitate such a move. But, natch, it was not to be. "That's too dangerous."

Ms Teffaha also crossed a red line by involving herself in the problem of child-stealing by CPS or other child safety agencies. I must be naive, since I figured she would have a chance of bringing the matter to a head. She is, after all, a solicitor. Oops, I mean she *was* a solicitor. A Queensland magistrate by the name of Judge Anthony Gett gave Ms Teffaha her walking papers. Technically, he referred her to the Victoria Legal Services Board which did the needful, but they would hardly override a judge.

Let's think about this for a minute. Serene Teffaha represented the people. She is much admired and loved. Should she be disbarred? Naturally, some behaviors warrant a disbarring. We need to have a monitoring system, and we do. But it looks like Teffaha was doing the right thing and Gett was doing the wrong thing.

How would I know? Well, when it comes to the child-sex-trafficking racket I wasn't born yesterday. I am the author of a 2019 book entitled *Reunion: Judging the Family Court.* It compares a few countries around the world but is mainly about Oz. The word 'reunion' means "let's unite the moms, or in some cases, dads, who have been deprived of their child for years by the rotten Family Court system." My 2019 book quotes a retired attorney in criminal law, Maurice Kriss, as follows:

"I am the President of the National Child Protection Alliance of Australia. I joined the NCPA where I was asked to assist a number of mothers who had their children taken from them by the Family Court after reporting that their children had been sexually abused .... **I noticed a distinct pattern: the mothers were treated with abuse and disrespect.**

They were called liars and [were] accused of coaching their children to lie. The fact that very young children at the time were bleeding from the anus or vagina did not move police. ... It took me some time to realise that the mothers had lost their children from the moment they filled in a Form 4 reporting sexual abuse. I [Maurice Kriss] was accused of being ...crazy. The Myth of lying mothers was deeply entrenched in the community."

[Kriss quoted an ICL (an Independent Children's Lawyer)]:
"An ICL said to me "The judge will give your client three chances to agree with his orders. He will raise his hand and show three fingers, after each time he will ask you the same question three times, if your client does not agree she will lose her child, do you understand me?" The father was accused of anal penetration of his 3-year-old child, had one computer with 82,000 pornographic images on his computer. His Honour dismissed the pornographic material and other evidence. Raised his three fingers ...."

Magistrate Gett

I googled for "trust in the judiciary" and forgot to specify Australia, so the reply I received a Gallop poll from 2015 showing Seppo trust running at 53%. (Seppo is Aussie slang for Yankee):

"Americans' trust in the judicial branch of the federal government has fallen significantly in the past year, and now a record-low 53% say they have "a great deal" or "a fair amount" of trust in it." Now let me quote from Judge Terry Gardiner of Queensland:

“As magistrates we take an oath to... at all times and in all things do equal justice to all persons. All members of our community should feel as if they can trust in the judiciary to the highest degree.”

Indeed, high ideals and ethics go naturally with the practice of law. If there is a judge who does not get that point, he/she needs to be removed quickly.

I think Brisbane Magistrate Gett does not get the point. My trusted sources for this are Pastor Paul Robert Burton who witnessed Gett’s performance in court, and Pridgeon himself. Allow me to quote Pridgeon's book. There are three issues on which Gett let him down. The first has to do with false statements made about Pridgeon. [All bolding here is by MM]:

Issue One

“Sgt Darren Williamson of the AFP, the Federal Case Officer in this prosecution, **swore an affidavit dated 19 October 2018**, stating on page 5 that 'Financial records sho (sic) that the defendant [Pridgeon] has moved considerable assets offshore, having sold his residence, and in 2018 has transferring (sic) more than $1.3 million offshore since September 2017....'

"This false allegation was repeated in an Objection to Bail Affidavit Annexure on page 5 undated. This and other untruthful assertions about my having 'numerous citizenships' and that I 'may have access to false identities' in Williamson’s affidavit were successfully used to argue that I was a flight risk.”

This misinformation was the basis for Pridgeon to be subjected to onerous Bail Conditions. He had to report to the bail office daily for years, and wear an uncomfortable ankle bracelet. Locals reading Williamson's words in the newspaper may very well have believed that “criminal Pridgeon” was a flight risk.

But he was never a flight risk, as the AFP had custody of his passport. It was sheer harassment, meant to break him. He deduces the following, which sounds correct to me:

"I raised the conduct of the AFP formally with the CDPP and Magistrate Gett, without success: The Court apparently felt that they knew better than I whether or not Sgt Williamson … had recklessly and knowingly made false statements to the Court, and whether these false assertions were used to mislead the CDPP as well as the court. **They chose to ignore them, and thereby made themselves and the Magistrates Court complicit in the crime of Perjury."**

The current CDPP -- Commonwealth Director of Public Prosecutions -- is Scott Bruckard. He's been on board since 1987 and must have seen a lot in his day! His website says:

"The CDPP aims to contribute to a fair, safe, and just society by delivering an effective, independent prosecution service in accordance with the Prosecution Policy of the Commonwealth. We aim to: be fair, consistent and professional in everything we do."

(In my parish we would say "Mother of God!" to that, or possibly "Holy Mother of God.")

Issue Two

The second issue is much more serious. Pridgeon writes:
"I attempted to **hand up the Police Statement by S/Sgt Miles together with the Townsville CPIU video of the forensic interview during which Ben disclosed the abuse** by his father, to Magistrate Gett during a Directions Hearing. I presented this as evidence of the Police misfeasance during the irregular investigation of Ben's abuse. Magistrate Gett refused to accept it. **I was so taken aback by this I did not know what to say.**"

So here we have what is typical of cases where the mum reports sexual abuse by the father. The mum is then persecuted by police and courts while everything is done to keep Dad out of legal trouble. I think we can say that **Dad is under the guaranteed protection of the courts.** And this is why I point the finger at judges. They have the final say both as to the fate of the child and as to letting certain people get away with crimes against children.

In this case, a boy, codenamed Ben, was in a police tape-recorded interview accusing his father of abusing him (badly). The father is codenamed AF2 (for "abusive father" 2). The police suppressed this taped evidence for years — AS IS THEIR WONT — but someone sent Dr Pridgeon a USB of that interview. Pridgeon "sprung it in court" but to no avail. (You're getting the drift here?)

"We already had the Police Statement by S/Sgt David Miles stating that ['Ben,' a codename] had been interviewed 3 times **without disclosing abuse**, particularly by his father, so there it was: evidence that Miles had misled the courts. We repeatedly brought this before the Court, seeking to have the Court take notice of it and act as it should, … but gradually, I believe, we were placing these prosecutors in a more dangerous and untenable position."

The good doctor also needed to deploy the USB data about Ben as a way of refuting a defamation suit that AF2 filed against him:

"As I was presenting my submissions to the court, while I was pointing out the misfeasance of the Police and the Prosecutors, Magistrate Gett interrupted me and threatened me with Criminal Defamation if I proceeded further. [Now that's a definite Holy Mother of God right there.]

"I was astonished by this, and stupidly, still could not believe that a magistrate would misuse his position so blatantly. Everything that I was saying to the Court was provable from the evidence in the CDPP Brief, and Truth is an absolute defence against a charge of defamation. **This threat prevented me from presenting my defence** at the Committal."

Issue Three

The third issue involves Serene Teffaha, sort of. It's about the fact that the Prosecutor had indicted Pridgeon for such-and-such, but in the courtroom Magistrate Gett changed this. Per Russell:

"At the Committal, the CDPP withdrew the s363(1)(a) Child Stealing charges and said they were going to charge us with s363(1)(b): Harbouring or receiving a stolen child. At Magistrate

Gett's suggestion, the CDPP withdrew the charges and Magistrate Gett charged us with the new charge of Harbouring or receiving a stolen child.

"During their discussions, senior prosecutor advised the Magistrate that the changes to the charges were "substantial". The significance of this is that this obliged the CDPP to obtain fresh consents from the Director of the CDPP. This was never done.

"The change of charges at Committal meant that we had no chance to defend ourselves against the new charges, and we were given no notice of the changes in charges, **this was a planned ambush: we were compelled to file our submissions 6 months before the Committal hearing, the CDPP had no such restriction."**

Dr Pridgeon is as humanly vulnerable as the rest of us. He is looking at many years in jail. So he took advice about appealing:

"I made an application to appeal this to the High Court, hoping to find a Court in Australia that acted according to law. [Keep tryin', Boy.] Unfortunately, we were denied this, and so applied to the Supreme Court for Judicial Review. I did this as I believed that if the CDPP managed to herd us into a mass trial with my co-defendants' lawyers, who didn't appear to be trying to protect their clients at all, I would be placed in a vulnerable position."

Pridgeon has been self-representing ever since he went broke. Russell has had to buy a lot of petrol. He lives in NSW but must appear in Queensland court! (Oddly, there does not seem to be a satisfactory reason for his federal trial to be held in that state.)

Pridgeon writes in his 2023 book, *Everybody Knows:*
"My co-defendant, whose grandson was removed by Police action by **Det Snr Sgt David Miles' perjurious statement** to the Courts, was being assisted by a courageous, tireless and highly committed solicitor: Serene Teffaha, who, unlike the other solicitors had fought tooth and nail for her. Serene had also brought the misconduct to the Court's attention, by writing a letter to

Magistrate Gett, in a private communication. This Magistrate used my co-defendant's committal proceedings, in 2020, to publicly excoriate and humiliate her.

"In doing so he revealed the contents of Ms Teffaha's private communication [to him] to the public, including the attending journalists, in open court, while accusing her of bringing the administration of justice into disrepute. Gett then made a complaint to the Legal Services Board in Victoria against Serene. She was struck off directly.

"Thus the Criminal Enterprise that is Operation Noetic continues: and more than ever it is obvious that EVERYONE KNOWS. Definition: Noetic: relating to mental activity or the intellect; 'the noetic quality of a mystical experience refers to the sense of revelation.' A Freemasonry concept."

We should wonder if it is "feasible" for Sgt Darren Williamson to be brought to book. People unthinkingly note from news articles that a cop accused of, say, brutality, receives from his Boss an exoneration. "End of story. The guy was acting in accord with duty." But note the law maxim: *Nemo judex sua causa*: a man can't be judge in his own case.

I believe that if judges in Oz are paid to act for the bad guys, the real child stealers, it seems they are automatically disqualified from trying a case against any person for that crime. It would be like a double nemo-judex thing. Or to put it more bluntly, they should be disqualified from being judges at all.

Recapping this chapter: Retired attorney Maurice Kriss explained the three-fingered judge. Russell Pridgeon listed three failures of Magistrate Gett: 1. He wouldn't listen to a complaint that Sgt Darren Williamson lied about the doctor being a flight risk. 2. Gett didn't let Pridgeon proffer crucial evidence of Ben's abuse, as found in a statement by Sgt David Miles and in a video (which is also proof of police misfeasance). 3. A new charge was made at Committal, giving the defendant no time to prepare for it, plus Gett used Pridgeon's hearing to disbar Serene Teffaha.

Wonderfully, Russell states that the magistrate is complicit in the crimes of the DPP. By the way, Gett spent most of his career as a lawyer within the DPP. Clearly he wasn't prepared for a Russell.

4. But When Is Government Actually a Private Entity?

nswmc.org.au

Thirteen of the nineteen members of the NSW Medical Council.

For my money, one of the super-duper discoveries of the entire book, *Everybody Knows*, is Pridgeon's observation that the Medical Council is not the government. Of course there are many self-governing institutions in society. Some of them contain "authority." So you would naturally think that the behavior of those institutions is related to law and that they are answerable to someone higher up in government.

In 2012, I was researching the control of doctors in the US, for my book *Consider the Lilies: A Review of 18 Cures for Cancer and Their Legal Status.* I learned that each physician must obey his state's AMA rules as to "best practice." For cancer patients, she must order only the Big Three treatments — surgery, chemo, and radiation. Maybe she has located a cancer cure that does not fit the Big Three? Well, stiff biccies. If she insists on curing her patient, she'll be de-registered. And if sued, she hasn't a leg to stand on.

Look into the history of this, and you will see that each of the 50 state legislatures has bowed to pressure from the American Medical Association. Roughly, the state has imbued that private organization, the AMA, with authority. So when the cancer curer does her thing, she knows the AMA might take away her license. (If you look further back to 1920 or so, you will see that the

Rockefeller family overhauled Medicine. This involved the taking over of medical journals and medical schools.) Americans have no clue that government-type agencies wield *major* power.

Apart from his trial that I am covering in this book, Pridgeon had to deal with the Health Care Complaints Commissioner, the HCCC, as three complaints had been received about him. Two came from an abusive father, clearly for the purpose of harassing Pridgeon; the third came from the AFP police. To fight the complaints, he had to go to a tribunal of the Medical Council, where he lost, and then to the NSW Supreme Court, Court of Appeal where he won. I will outline that painful business here.

One of the dad's two complaints was that Russell had given a lady 3 pages off his prescription pad, telling her to get what she likes. Seems preposterous, but how should the HCCC react? Choices under sec 145B (1) of the *Health Care Complaints Act* of 1993 are:

"(a) the Council may make any inquiries about the complaint the Council thinks appropriate; (b) the Council may refer the complaint to the Commission for investigation; ...((j) the Council may determine that no further action should be taken ...."

The dad's claim about the prescription-pad thing occurred 15 years ago, so clearly it was not worth anything. I will mention his second complaint later.

Another moan from Russell was the lack of speed in handling the complaints. He made many attempts to learn the status of the prescription-pad complaint. He notes that:

"The legislation orders the HCCC to act with speed and efficiency: Section 29A of the Act directs the HCCC to act "expeditiously", there is a similar clause in the Health Practitioners Regulation National Law....Eventually, in November 2022, after more than four years, I was advised that this complaint was closed."

A note on activism: it was treatment like this, received by Bill Windsor in a civil case in Georgia that caused him to initiate the

Lawless America series on YouTube, in which we find the Mona Gudbranson testimony. She mentioned that her daughter Ingrid was tied up constantly attending hearings and faithfully carrying out any mission she was given by the Family Court.

In both American and Australian law, it's possible to file tort suits, per common law. One tort is "The intentional infliction of emotional distress." An example is threatening someone. All the protective parents are under this kind of stress, and their lawyer is likely to tell them (correctly) that they may lose the child forever.

The AFP Gets Russell's Medical License Removed

The AFP complaint was a standard report to the medical council (connected to the HCCC as a co-regulator) that Pridgeon had been arrested. Recall that Operation Noetic had swooped down, on 'Kingpin' Pridgeon, on 17 October 2018. He was arrested on the 17th, spent three nights in the Watchhouse, got bail – and went back to work on the 22nd.

Soon, the Medical Council took away his right to practice medicine. Personally, I think it would be reasonable for the Medical Council to do that to a man arrested for child-trafficking -- if it meant he was actually buying and selling kids, not helping a mum rescue her own daughters. But the AFP did know Russell was not 'caught' in a crime. He had volunteered to them, 5 months earlier, what he was doing, and asked for their help for the kids.

Russell thinks, and I agree, that the Noetic persecution is not so much about him but rather to let everyone out there know what will happen to them if they get, um, pushy. "Never be pushy. Just bow and obey. Oh, and don't go around starting Anti-Paedophile Political Parties, hear?" (O'Dea was also a founder of that Party.)

The Accountability of the Medical Council

The Medical Council is composed of 19 persons, according to their website nswmc.org.au, as retrieved on May 1, 2023. Of their 19 members, 6 are appointed by the Minister for Health, including one 1 legal practitioner, another 2 by the Australian Medical

Association, 9 by groups (colleges) of specialists, 1 by Multicultural NSW, and 1 by the universities of Sydney and Newcastle, jointly. How a college, such as the College of Obstetrics, picks its member might be an interesting sidelight.

The big question is: To whom is the MC accountable? I assume they are funded by the state, as they make an annual financial report to parliament, per the Statutory Bodies Act of 1964 and the Public Finance and Audit Act of 1963. But it is my guess that they are controlled by the Powers That Be -- whether the cabal, the mafia, Mr Global, or whoever really runs the show. Like the AMA in US, they are outside democracy as they are unaccountable.

Russell brought his best arguments to the tribunal but the tribunal members gave no relief. The name of the tribunal is NCAT, a Civil Administrative Tribunal. In my opinion they were tasked with frustrating Russell and continuing to prevent him from making a living as a doctor, which was, naturally, demoralizing.

The Medical Council's biggest hit on Russell -- surely he can sue for defamation -- consisted of an item they wrote in the file accusing him of being a pedophile. In the dad's complaint, that dad had never suggested in any way that Russell ever abused any child. In his book *Everybody Knows*, Pridgeon says:

"I wrote a letter to Ms Rebecca Moynihan of the NSW Medical Council ... on 30 May 2021, and did not receive a reply. When I made my second appeal to the Medical Council, their submissions referred to [the dad's] complaint, saying that the complaint alleged that I had been accused of child sexual abuse: They said: "In the Chronology prepared by the Medical Council of NSW ... we see on Page 3 of the submissions for the section 150 proceedings: 'Dr Pridgeon is also accused of abusing the male child [Redacted name].'

"There was no allegation that I abused any child made in [the dad's] complaint, not even obliquely. The New South Wales Medical Council fabricated this allegation all by themselves."

The chapter at hand is meant to air out the important matter of government having within it some official-looking bodies whose allegiance is to an entity other than the nation. This needs to be taught in schools, so we don't create false hope of getting justice. Or to put it the other way, so we know that have to find better means of getting justice.

I propose that the entire scheme that I call "KK" be thrown out. Those who suffered under it (protective parents, kids, and some cops and lawyers) should come forward with their stories. *Pro tem*, they can use aliases such as Jane Doe, Baby Doe, Cop Doe.

They can each sue a relevant person for IED, Intentional infliction of emotional distress! It has never been possible for any one of them to prove that there was "intention," but the conglomerate is proof. It is beyond doubt that a plan is in place to lower the mother's confidence and dignity, and to drive her crazy with the frustration and expense of the ordeal, not to mention being called a liar and knowing that her child is also being branded a lair.

It is also worth having an investigation of the hiring of hitmen which surely does go on. Hitmen perform such tasks as poisoning the pets of a trouble-making protective parent, slashing tires of whistleblowers' cars, and fiddling with their bank accounts.

And let's find out who trains court personnel to look happy at a ruling against a mother. Mona Gudbranson said the court personnel were doing high-fives when Ingrid lost her children. I know of a similar thing happening in Adelaide, with the female magistrate smiling like a basket of chips. But lawsuits for torts aren't enough if there are crimes being committed. Some prosecutions could arise right now -- in the O'Dea and Pridgeon case alone.

I got my best sense of what Russell has suffered when I read, in his book, how he felt when the Court of Appeal restored his license:

"It was a wonderful relief to return to work, and very healing."

5. The True-Blue Scoop on Section 70NAE. Don't Miss It!

A happy child, Photo: Leo Rivas, Nikon, under the Unsplash Agreement

This chapter won't discuss the case of The King versus O'Dea and Pridgeon. It is about the 2015 case of **Argyle v Thomas**. It is a hum dinger. Honestly, you may think it must be a satire.

It gives major insight -- horrible insight -- into the way a judge can reverse reality so as to blame a mum for what a dad does. He can do that while using the black-letter law known as The Family Law Act of 1975. It is administered federally, except in WA. The nice bits, happy bits, are in Sections 60 and 70. Let's go there first:

Sec 60CC says, that in deciding what is in the best interests of the child, in order "to make a particular parenting order… the court must consider: (2) (a) the **benefit to the child of having a meaningful relationship with both of the child's parents** [very good, we all need a Mum and Dad] and (b) …the need to **protect the child from physical or psychological** harm from being subjected to, or exposed to, abuse, neglect, or family violence." Wonderful.

But **that's a tall order**. Any layperson can see that **subsections (a) and (b) contradict each other**. If the parents do not live together, and one of them subjects the kid to abuse, how can the other parent, even if saintlike, with good intentions, see to it that the kid has a meaningful relationship with the abuser? It cannot be done. It would take miraculous powers for anyone to do it. So how do the courts overcome that juxtaposition? I believe the IN-HOUSE court rule is that a judge must deem '(a)' to be more of a guidance than '(b).' In short, they toss (b) to the winds. I place the blame for this legislative error on the judiciary, insofar as you never hear of the judiciary **pointing out to Parliament** that the a/b problem calls for a re-wording of the statute.

But don't take it from me that there is something underhanded going on. Take it from cases such as the one presented below. It's the 2017 ruling by a Federal judge in Sydney **that word-picks in the typical way**. The mother's case was lost even though "Dad had done a wee in me" because **it was foreordained that the judge was not going to find in the mother's behalf.** (So say I.)

Rather, he was going to: 1. order the visits to dad to continue, and 2. adjudicate against mum for contravening the parenting order, and also "award costs." (That is, make her pay the dad's lawyer for these various court hearings.)

Oops wait, wait, hold your horses, Everybody! **I also mentioned Section 70** of the FLA. Ah, goody! That's where we get into the fact that in some instances a parent SHOULD steal the child, for a specific time period. It's the famous subsection 70NAE.

It says you **may** contravene a parenting order if: (4)(a) the respondent believed on reasonable grounds that the actions constituting the contravention [e.g., hiding her kids in a warehouse] **were necessary to protect the health or safety of a person.** Whew! There's a way out for kids who are suffering and may grow up permanently damaged if no one rescues them. Thank God.

Um. Not so fast. For that to happen, **judges would have to apply** that law — 70NAE. But they don't. I'm willing to bet substantial rubles that you can't find a precedent where NAE saved the day. Even if the protective parent arrives in court armed with the exact, above-quoted wording, she won't see it used. She will leave that day's hearing completely dumbfounded at how a judge can eviscerate, water down, or waltz around NAE.

Or how the judge can just busy his tongue with distracting commentary. Funnily enough, he doesn't blush or stammer. It's as smooth as if he were reciting a railway timetable.

How did I locate this case? Easy. I went to the website of the Australian Legal Information Institute, at austlii.edu.au, and typed "70NAE" into the search box. First I got Enright & Shenk, and then: *Argyle & Thomas.* (The ampersand is used in Australian cases in place of the "v" for versus. An Oz abortion case would have been called Roe & Wade.) The court provides pseudonyms in Family Law cases: "Argyle" is the dad and "Thomas" the mum. If you are a law student, you MUST read it and you MUST **go to the dean to complain**. What an outrageous interpretation of the law. Who does Judge Brana Obradovic think she is! This case shows the KK system (Chapter 2 above) written in the stars.

****

Argyle v Thomas FCCA 621 [Federal Circuit Court of Australia] [all bolding added by MM] **Decided 2017,** Cases cited:

Searle & Mellor [2017] FamCAFC 46
Taikato v R [1996] HCA 28; (1996) 186 CLR 454
Childres v Leslie [2008] FamCAFC 5; (2008) FLC 93-356
In the marriage of O'Brien [1992] FamCA 52; (1993) FLC 92-396
Stamp & Stamp [2014] FCCA 1269
Raider & Raider [2011] FamCA 488
Vaughton & Randle (No.2) [2013] FamCA 286 [I'd look these up.]

ORDERS

(1) That a finding be recorded that the Respondent, without reasonable excuse, contravened the orders of the Federal Circuit Court made on 7 October 2014 in that:

(c) The Respondent without reasonable excuse failed to bring the children to school on 22 September 2016. The Respondent failed to communicate with the Applicant that the children would be absent from school and that as such alternative arrangements would have needed to be made to enable the Applicant to pick

up the children for his scheduled visit in adherence of the orders made 7 October 2014.
The Respondent failed to respond to the Applicant's attempts to contact the Respondent to find out the whereabouts of his children. The Respondent's actions on the above occasion are in contravention of Order 3, in particular (3)(II)(b).

•

FEDERAL CIRCUIT COURT OF AUSTRALIA [Sydney]
Relevant Facts The father was born on (omitted) 1974. The mother was born on (omitted) 1975. The parties were married on (omitted) 2007 and they separated in or about June 2012. The parties are yet to be divorced. There are three children of the parties: [ages 5, 7, and 9]

On 7 October 2014 final parenting orders were made by consent in the Federal Circuit Court of Australia ("Final Orders"). Relevantly, those Orders provided that the children are to live with the father, *inter alia,* during school term: a. each alternate Friday from after school and concluding at 5pm Sunday; and b. each alternate Thursday from after school to 9am Saturday.

From October 2014 until about mid-September 2016, the children, by and large, lived with each of the parents in accordance with the Final Orders. On Thursday, 8 September 2016 at 3pm, the father attended (omitted) Public School to collect the children at the commencement of their time with the father in accordance with the Final Orders. On 20 September 2016 the father voluntarily (and against legal advice) participated in an electronically recorded interview with the Police regarding the allegation of assaults on the children alleged by the mother against the father. The father denied that he physically assaulted the children and gave an account of the children's busy weekend with him including attending a children's (hobbies omitted).

The father also denied giving the children medication to sleep or that he banged the children's heads together. The Police records show that the **Police were of the view that there was insufficient evidence to proceed by way of charge and insufficient evidence to make an application for an Apprehended Violence Order.** [an AVO]

On 11 October 2016 the father received a telephone call from (omitted) Police in relation to a complaint they received from the mother, that the father had installed a GPS tracking device in a motor vehicle which the father purchased but then transferred to the wife in August 2016. The father agreed to participate in an interview with the Police. At the conclusion of that interview the father was told by the Police that no charges would be pressed and that he was free to go.

Tendered in the proceedings were a number of documents produced under Subpoena from the children's school, from FaCS, from the Police and from the Children's Hospital. Some of these documents have been specifically referred to in these Reasons, and while all have been considered by the Court not all were relevant to the discrete issue before the Court being the **mother's "reasonable excuse" argument.**

While all reasonable efforts have been made in these Reasons to refer to relevant evidence, not all of the evidence in the proceedings has been traversed with a fine-tooth comb in these Reasons. The Court is comforted in its approach by what the Full Court has recently said in *Searle & Mellor*:
"When dealing with large bodies of evidence, economy and/or truncation of expression and approach may be required to coherently explain the resolution of an overall controversy." [Ahem.]

The Law dealing with Contraventions. The relevant legislative provisions dealing with contraventions of parenting orders are found in Part VII Division 13A *Family Law Act 1975* (Cth). 23 b Varying parenting orders, which can be regarded as the least punitive response to the problem: subdivision B;
Contravention alleged but not established – provision for costs orders against the person bringing the proceedings: subdivision C; Contravention established, but a reasonable excuse – the Court can make orders for compensation for time lost, and costs orders: subdivision D;
Less serious contraventions, and no reasonable excuse – the Court has various powers, for example orders for compensation

for time lost, orders for post-separation parenting programs, bonds, and costs: subdivision E;

More serious contraventions, and no reasonable excuse – the Court has more punitive powers, including fines and imprisonment: subdivision F The meaning of "contravened an order" is set out in s70NAC of the *Family Law Act 1975* (Cth):

A person is taken for the purposes of this Division to have **contravened** an order under this Act affecting children if, and only if: (a) where the person is bound by the order – he or she has:
(i) intentionally failed to comply with the order; or
(ii) made no reasonable attempt to comply with the order;

...The mother admitted the contraventions. Therefore, the **onus of proof** shifted to the mother to establish that she had a reasonable excuse for the contraventions. The mother submitted that she had a reasonable excuse pursuant to 70NAE(5)(a) and (b).

Reasonable Excuse
[MM Interruption. There is a lot here and maybe you can't be bothered. But, I assure you, it is a gem. Judge Obradovic is going to play with words to assure that the kid continues to be abused. I've bolded your absolute minimum reading of this awful ruling.]

*The meaning of "reasonable excuse" is, relevantly, found in of the Act, which reads:
(1) The circumstances in which a person may be taken to have had, for the purposes of this Division, a reasonable excuse for contravening an order under this Act affecting children include, but are not limited to,
A reasonable excuse in respect of a concern as to the welfare of the child, is limited to a belief, on reasonable grounds, that depriving a person of time with a child pursuant to an order was necessary to protect the health and safety of a person. It is not a question as to whether in the view of the parent with whom a child lives, or in the view of that parent on reasonable grounds, that the carrying out of the order might not be in the best interests

of the child. **The question is whether it is necessary to protect the health or safety of a person including the child.** [Fine.]

Section 70NAEwas considered by Warnick J in *Childers & Leslie* where his Honour said: … **The question is not simply whether, viewed from some ill-defined concept of fairness or reasonableness, the mother's actions were excusable.** [??] The position with regard to the terms "reasonable grounds" and "reasonable excuse" in s 70NAE is, I think, similar to that of terms of like generality, for example, "any just cause" used elsewhere in the Act. As Lindemayer J said of the term "any just cause" in In the Marriage of Lutzke [1979] FamCA 60; (1979) 5 FamLR 553 at 559:

… However, the Act is silent as to what may constitute "just cause" for the discharge of an order. **In my opinion, however, the words "just cause" are not used in any broad general sense, nor are they intended to import any abstract notions of justice....**

[MM -- Law student, are you getting your Dean Speech ready?]

Here, the context in which "reasonable excuse" applied tellingly included the subsections of s 70NAE. It also included that the father was entitled to spend time with the child pursuant to a court order. Such an order **places serious obligations on persons in the position of the mother in this case.** [Agreed.]

The Mother's Case [We are in Thomas v Argyle here]
The mother's evidence is that on 4 September 2016 she picked the children up after they had spent time with the father in accordance with the Final Orders and that on the way home the children said to her that the father had smacked them. ... when they got home and when the mother asked what happened and what is it that the father did, Y **showed the mother a bruise on her knee and Z showed the mother a bruise on his thigh.** The children then apparently started to cry and Y said to the mother that the father hit the children with his belt and slippers, that he carried Z under his arm and **threw him on the bed and that Z hit the back of his head on Y's head.**

X said she was told by the father not to make any noise because **he was tutoring** in the other room and that he gets angry if the children make noise. Y then said to the mother that she had a headache. It appears from the mother's evidence that the children were all together when these conversations were occurring.

The mother says that she **was in shock and concerned about the children's safety.** She called the Department of Family and Community Services that evening [big mistake] when the children went to bed and reported her concerns. The following day she called (omitted) Police and made a complaint that the father had been hitting the children and that she was therefore concerned for their safety. The Police attended the mother's home later that day. The mother's evidence is that she said to the Police:

"The children came home from their father's house on Sunday and were upset. They said that their dad hit them and threw them on the bed. They are complaining of headaches now. **I don't know what to do. I am scared he will hurt them again**."

What the mother says she said to the Police is not what she says the children said to her. It is at the very least, an exaggeration. There was no complaint **that all of** the children had been thrown on the bed or that they were **all** complaining of headaches. Furthermore, at the time that the Police were at the mother's house, she received a call from the school to say that Y was sick and that she was complaining of a headache.

The mother then took the children to their General Practitioner ('GP') at (omitted) Medical Centre. It appears that all of the children were together with the mother and the GP, and that they said to the GP words to the effect of "daddy smacks us and gives this medicine before we go to bed".

The GP then apparently said to the mother that he had to call the Department of Family and Community Services as the children had already complained to him that the father had given them 'poison medicine' before.
Such evidence is extraordinary. [What does the judge mean?]

The mother, unfortunately, was not cross-examined about this particular evidence. **The Court does not say that as a criticism of Counsel for the father** who cross-examined the mother at length in relation to some very important matters. It is noted simply because there was **no exploration of the issue** that more than likely the child had been sick and that was why she had the headache – rather than any **inference such as the one that the mother appears to have drawn, that the reason that she had a headache is because of some abuse** that she had suffered....

The discharge of referral from the hospital says that the child Y presented to the hospital with an injury, being a soft tissue injury. The discharge referral then notes as follows:

"[Y] Was in care of father over the weekend. Mother noticed in bath last night new bruises and Y was c/o headache. **Mother has footage on her phone of the children and telling her that the father hit them several times with belt buckle and threw them on to the mattress, hitting side of bed/colliding heads.**

Third child oldest girl was not hit by father. Children state that he "loves" her – mother tells me that he licks her ear and snuggles with her in bed. Ongoing for many years."

Previous AVOs against father, now elapsed, GP has apparently reported to FACS as has mother on multiple other occasions. Mother found a GPS tracker in her car, notes cars following her, Never been to hospital before for injuries Y has had headache since Saturday. No visual changes, vomiting, dizziness.

Running around examination room – mother states they are always "hyperactive" the two days after returning from father's care

Bruising noted over pre-tibial area, one bruise right buttock, patch of discolouration/dry skin low thoracic spin. Says "ouch" on palpation over entire spine and long bones, smiling throughout.

[Reader, please stick with this. I continue with the judge's ruling. All is quote of the case. Only square-bracket stuff is mine. -- MM]

Once again the matters noted in the discharge referral do not strictly accord with the other evidence in the proceedings. For example, the mother's evidence is that Y complained about having a headache *"now"* being after she returned from spending time with the father on the Sunday, **rather than having a headache all weekend.**

If what is recorded in the discharge referral is correct, namely that Y has had a headache since Saturday, **then what the mother says in her Affidavit is deliberately misleading. The Court is of the view that it is more probable than not**, given that the child came home sick from school on Monday with a headache, that she had had a headache since Saturday and that the headache was **related to an illness, rather than any alleged abuse at the hands of the father.**

The mother says that she was advised approximately three weeks later by (omitted) Police that the decision had been taken to close the investigation. The mother asserts **that the Police officer who spoke to her said words to the effect "*there was nothing wrong with Mr Argyle hitting the children.*"** The mother then gives the following evidence:

"…I was concerned for the children's safety if I let them go to Mr Argyle's house and did not think the police were taking the investigation seriously. "
"I was concerned that if Mr Argyle pick the children up from school and had them for the weekend that he would hit them again. I thought that the children were not safe staying with their father overnight. I decided to keep the children at home on 8 September 2016, 16 September 2016 and 22 September 2016 **as I thought that this was in the children's best interest.**"

The mother's Affidavit then goes on to explain that since the Final Orders she had been concerned that the father has been **inappropriate with X**. The mother goes on to say:

a. That in or around January 2015, **X told her** that the father "*did a wee in me.*" The mother apparently went to the Family Court at Parramatta "*to try and put a stop to the final orders*" where she spoke to a Duty Solicitor and was told that she had to make a report to the Police as it was "*too late.*" The mother went to Police were [sic] X was questioned by the Police, the mother also made a complaint to FaCS and a social worker from FaCS also interviewed X.

b. That since the Final Orders "X would return from her father's house with redness in her vagina. **X would find it very difficult and painful to walk.** I tried to ask X how this happened but she would not reply. Since she stopped going to her father's house on 4 September 2016, the redness stopped."

That since the Final Orders she has not only witnessed the father licking X's ear, but that she asked the father to stop and not do it again to which the father replied that he is not doing anything wrong.

It appears that **no action was taken** by the Police or FaCS in relation to the complaint made by the mother that the father **had *'weed'* in X**, at the time the complaints were made or since.

The mother was cross-examined at length by Counsel for the father about the various complaints she made to Police in September 2016.

It is clear from the oral evidence of the mother and the documents produced under Subpoena from New South Wales Police which were ultimately tendered, **that the mother did not mention any redness of the vagina** relating to Y until 13 September 2016 [so?], and that after she was told by the Police that they would not be applying for an Apprehended Violence Order against the father that she repeated to the Police the older complaints about the father doing a *"wee"* in X. [Anybody listening?]

The mother also made a number of other complaints on that occasion including that the father showers with the children, that he sleeps with the children by pushing three single beds together and that X sits on the father's lap and his genitals.]

Certainly the mother does not say that this was a reason why the children did not spend time with the father on the dates the subject of the contravention. [Well, yes she does, really.] In any event, **the Police have not taken any action against the father as a result of the complaints made by the mother** on

13 September 2016 relating to conduct of an alleged sexual nature by the father towards the children and particularly X.

The mother further says that since the Final Orders the children had expressed to her that they did not want to go to the father's house and that they had told her that he scared them and asked the mother not to make them go to spend time with the father. When the children were said to have said that these things is **not the subject of any evidence.** [Yoo-hoo, Your Honor.]

The mother also makes further complaints X has started to wet herself, that Y started to wet the bed at night and that all three children see a Counsellor. The mother also says that in September 2016 during the time that the children did not see their father they stopped wetting the bed. The mother states that since the children started seeing the father again they have started to wet the bed again.
These matters namely the children's apparent reluctance to spend time with the father or their incontinence issues, were not raised by the mother during submissions as a basis of her reasonable excuse argument.

Distress of a child may give rise to a claim of reasonable excuse, if it results in risk of harm to the child's emotional wellbeing. It has been said that:

Analysis and Conclusion. The wording of s70NAE(5) was referred to earlier in these Reasons. Section 70NAE(5) was considered by Dawe J in Vaughton & Randle where it was held that: (82) There are multiple considerations, both **subjective** and objective, involved in applying subsection 70NAE(5) to the facts.

(83) **First, there is the issue of whether the respondent believed on reasonable grounds that not allowing the child and the applicant to spend time together was necessary to protect the health and safety of the child.** This issue has a subjective element (consideration of whether the respondent **actually** believed that not allowing the child and the applicant to spend time together was necessary to protect the health and safety of the child) and an **objective** element (consideration of whether this belief of the respondent was **reasonable**). [Dear God.]

(84) Second, there is the consideration of whether the period during which the child and the person did not spend time together was "longer than was necessary to protect the health or safety" of the child pursuant to s 70NAE(5)(b). (Original emphasis) With these remarks, the Court respectfully agrees. **They are a statement of the law** which applies to this case.

The Court does not accept that there were reasonable grounds for the mother to believe that the children had been physically abused by the father, despite what she says the children had said to her. [And the recorded calls?] The mother complained to the Police. The Police did not take any action against the father as a result of the complaints **they did not even apply for an Apprehended Violence Order.** The mother took the children to be examined by the Children's Hospital. There was **nothing sinister** reported by the doctors who examined the children, indeed the children were observed to be playing happily and **Y was observed to be smiling while complaining of pain.**

The Court finds that the mother has **not established the defence of 'reasonable excuse'** within the meaning of s70 NAE(5) in respect of any of the counts. The Court reiterates the long standing authority that parents **have obligations to comply with orders for children to spend time** with the other parent.

Conclusion [by judge]. **Lest it be suggested** that it was not considered, the Court finds that the **cumulative** effect of the facts as found is not such that there were reasonable grounds for mother **to hold a belief** that withholding the children from the father, was necessary to **protect the health** or safety of the children.

****

Dear Reader, the above is not a one-off judgment: it is ***commonplace***. I hope you agree with me that such rulings in file must not be allowed to stand. *Argyle v Thomas* needs to be reopened, at least by a law student acting unofficially, but preferably by an act of Parliament calling for the complete inspecting of any 70NAE case coming from that judge or any other judge. This is murder and murder has no statute of limitations. Even when something is outside the "statute of lim," that's not God speaking -- it is a *statute* and Parliament has every ability to amend it. Legislatures should also say that diagnosing the mum with Munchausen-by-proxy syndrome, must not be invoked as this is not a medical illness.

Before closing this crucial chapter, I should mention that much of the decision making by magistrates in Australia, working hand in glove with CPS, takes place in Children's Courts rather than Family Law Court. There, due process is *officially* negligible; rules of evidence are not used. And all this chicanery relies on another famous part of the Family Law Act, sec 121, that gags everybody. Sec 121 has prevented many a protective parent from being able to get help from the public. He or she lives in no small fear of being arrested for contempt of court if any beans get spilled!

Also, please be aware that the ruling in Argyle could just as well have been made in any American case. See the National Women's Coalition for umpteen such rulings in the US. It looks like the agenda is installed worldwide. Is it possible that all government people have been told what to do? Are they programmed?

On July 26, 2018, *Forbes* magazine ran an article by Tara Haelle, about Air Force Colonel Eric Holt, whose twin sons claim assault by him. It says: "The boys repeatedly returned from visits with their father with bruises, lacerations and genital injuries that research suggests are unlikely to have been accidental during usual child play." Haelle notes that the military could have court-martialed the dad, but they did not even call him to a preliminary Article 32 hearing. Congress has a say in military discipline, but petitions to Rep Joseph Kennedy and others in Holt's case were not effective. The mom was treated per the standard script.

To conclude Part One, I reiterate a suggestion from my book *Reunion* that we organize reunions for all the relevant children.
I wrote the following song when an Australian mum got an unexpected chance to reunite. Tune and lyrics are public domain:

***End of Part One: Breakthrough* / / Song for a Reunion with Mum.** Sing it to the tune of "On the Road to Gundagai." Note for singers: bolding means emphasis on this syllable.

The memories always there of those dear days. How I loved to watch my child and see her **ways**./ You **know I'm always** yearnin', just to be returnin'/ And to have a real re-**union** with my girl…./Let's get **back**, on the track, we can **do** without the flack/And be **unit**ed once again.

Refrain: Oh, when I see her growin', the tears will be a-flowin'/ Beneath a sunny sky./ She has **gone** now to school, and **acquired** some pals./ I don't know what she… even re***mem***bers of me/ But we'll soon revive the past, And I **know** it's going to last/ When I **cuddle** my **ba**by again.

2. When we **meet,** the years of **hurt** will disappear/ Unfairness, begone! It's time to indulge in cheer/ The dreams will be abounding, and all the love resounding/It'll be heaven for Mom, and **joy for** the child./ We'll be back, on the track. Pay no attention to the flack!/ We'll be **united** once again./ Refrain: Oh, when I see her growin', tears will be a-flowin'....

GumshoeNews.com readers commented on the above song:
Diane DeVere: A mother's heartbeat. Breaking the cycle of generational trauma -- may it be a wondrous reunion full of love and healing.

Fair Dinkum: I'm sending a horde of good angels, or however many are out there paying the slightest attention to me... towards that mum's direction.... In the name of all things right! (And maybe smite the any and all that deserve a good smiting while they're there….)

The actual mum in this case did not see her girl for 8 years.

Sir Wm Blackstone *Judge Bruce Ermine* *Sir Edward Coke*

Good day, attendees of this session of the Brisbane District Court. I am Judge Ermine. The case before us is The King versus Blah Blah and Blah Blah. The prosecutor for Queensland, please stand, is Miss Karen Grace Brumby. The defendants, please stand, are self-representing. Please be seated.

Audio recording is permitted; photographing is prohibited. As one of the defendants is hard of hearing. I have ordered a screen to placed in front of him with an instant printout of what is being said. If it fails to work, he may signal the bailiff.

This is the people's court and it is also the king's court, and right now it is my court. The most important person, or entity, in this room, is the Law. Australian law — largely inherited from England as the common law — knows what it's doing. The law has taken centuries to perfect itself. Many fine minds, some seemingly inspired, have contributed. And it remains for Parliament to continue to adjust the law, by statute, by amendment, or by repeal.

Nevertheless, every case also contributes to the ongoing construction of the common law. This will be one such case. In this courtroom we will all show respect for the law and for the two sides, the prosecution and the defense.

It would not be right for you to say that the defendants deserve less respect because they are criminals. They are not criminals at this moment. They are citizens charged with a crime. At the end of this court case, it may be that they will be called criminals, if the jury convicts them.

One way for the persons in the gallery to show respect is by being quiet. I will take it to be criminal contempt of court if anyone interrupts this session. I will cite you for contempt. The state police, who are standing outside the building, will arrest you.

However, it may be that you, as citizens, have something important to tell me. I will give you an opportunity for that later on. As for the media, a few of whose members are here today, I greet you as honorable reporters. If you intentionally misreport what has gone on in this courtroom, I will cite you for contempt.

I am told that distinct misreporting of this case by mainstream media has been going on for four years, creating injustice in the lives of the defendants. Why would anyone do that?

To begin now, I shall describe the court's role in making justice happen, and I thank the members of the jury for being here to make this possible. There are two kinds of cases. One is civil law, also known as private law. Because members of society often have conflicts with one another they can bring their civil case to court for resolution. The other kind of case is criminal law.

Such cases do not have an individual aggrieved party. When any person disobeys any law, the aggrieved party is the whole society. Society needs to have law enforced, for the good of all. The state will prosecute the lawbreaker on behalf of society. Who will win? Truth will win. Truth is perhaps the greatest human achievement and a court is tasked with guarding it.

Everyone in this courtroom, especially the jurors, should want the state of Queensland to outline clearly what the law is and how Messrs Blah Blah and Blah Blah may have broken it. Appropriate evidence should be shown and witnesses may appear.

They will be examined and then cross-examined by the other party. The defendants should also state clearly how they did not break the law and may call witnesses to testify.

As it happens, the crimes with which today's defendants are charged are: perversion of the course of justice, and conspiracy to pervert the course of justice. An English writer, Sir William Blackstone, said in his *Commentaries on the Laws of England*, in 1769, that crimes against justice are worthy of punishment — clearly, it is everyone's duty to protect the law, as such. I will quote from him now to help us rejoice in the law.

From Volume 4 of Blackstone's Commentaries. I will read ten of what he lists as "offenses against public justice."

1. VACATING records**, or falsifying certain other proceedings in a court of judicature**, is a felonious offense against public justice. It is enacted by statute of Henry the Sixth, that if any clerk, or other person, shall willfully take away, withdraw, or avoid any record, **or process** in the superior courts of justice in Westminster-hall, … **it is felony not only in the principal actors, but also in their abettors**.

2. OBSTRUCTING **the execution of lawful process** is at all times an offense of a very high and presumptuous nature; And it has been held, that the party opposing such arrest [of a criminal] becomes thereby an accessory in felony, and a **principal in high treason**.

3. BREACH of prison by the offender himself was felony at the common law: But this severity is mitigated by the statute *de frangentibus prisonam* of King Edward the Second, which enacts, that no person shall have **judgment of life or member** [imagine it -- member!], for breaking prison, unless committed for some capital offense.

4. The RECEIVING of stolen goods, knowing them to be stolen, is also a high misdemeanor and affront to public justice. There is also the offense of *theft-bote*, which is where the party robbed not

only knows the felon, but also takes his goods **upon agreement not to prosecute**. This perversion of justice, in the old Gothic constitutions, was liable to the most severe and infamous punishment.

5. BARRETRY is the offense of frequently exciting and stirring up suits and quarrels between his majesty's subjects, either at law or otherwise.... **if the offender belongs to the profession of the law**, he ought to be disabled from practicing for the future. ...and [pay] treble damages to the party injured.

6. COMPOUNDING informations upon penal statutes [today, the stacking up of charges] contributes to making the laws odious to the people. At once therefore **to discourage malicious informers,** it is enacted by Queen Elizabeth that if any person, informing under pretense of any penal law, shall **stand two hours on the pillory**.

7. A CONSPIRACY also **to indict an innocent man of felony falsely and maliciously**, is a farther abuse and perversion of public justice; for which the party injured were by the ancient common law to receive what is called the villainous judgment; *viz.,* to have those perpetrators lands wasted, **their houses razed,** and their trees rooted up.

8. PERJURY and suborning it. The next offense against public justice is **the crime of willful and corrupt perjury**; which is defined by Sir Edward Coke, to be a crime committed when a lawful oath is administered, in some judicial proceeding, to a person who swears falsely, in a matter material to the point in question. Subornation of perjury is the offense of procuring another to take such a false oath.... The punishment was anciently death; then banishment, or **cutting out the tongue**, and now it is fine and imprisonment. But for the suborner of perjury, Queen Elizabeth inflicts the penalty of **perpetual infamy** and to stand **with both ears nailed to the pillory**.

9. BRIBERY is the next species of offense against public justice; which is **when a judge, or other person concerned in the**

administration of justice, takes any undue reward to influence his behavior in his office. … In England this offense of taking bribes is punished with fine and imprisonment. But in judges, especially the superior ones, it has been always looked upon as so heinous an offense, that **Chief Justice Thorpe was hanged for it** in the reign of Edward the Third.

10. THE POWER and wealth of the offenders may often **deter the injured from [seeking] a legal prosecution**. This is yet another offense against public justice, and is a crime of deep malignity.

Indeed. Neither power nor wealth will influence my court. Now let us proceed. Ms Prosecutor, what have you to say?

Your Honor, may I approach the Bench?

Judge Ermine: Yes.

Prosecutor Karen Grace Brumby: I need to consult the DPP, Your Honor. May I step outside for a few minutes to make a phone call?

Judge Ermine: Certainly.

Prosecutor Brumby (whispering to the judge): Having heard what I may be up for, I am going to tender my resignation.

Judge: That may be wise.

7. Internal Judicial Reform Is Inauspicious (i.e., Hopeless)

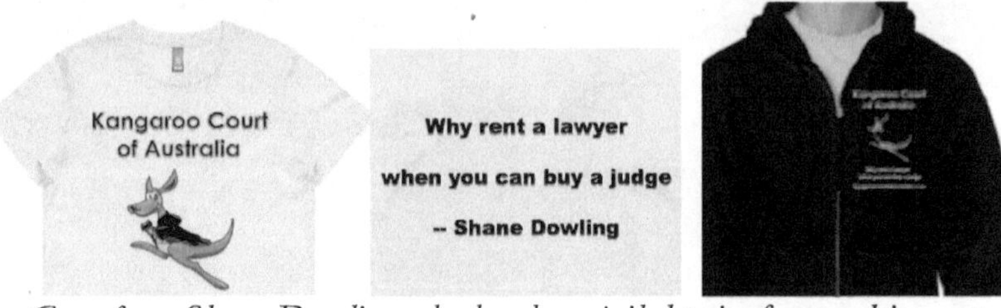

Gear from Shane Dowling who has been jailed twice for speaking out

Now we can get back to the subject of the "child-stealing" case of Patrick O'Dea and Dr Russell Pridgeon. It was due to begin today, 7 June, but has been pushed off till November 2023. The handling of the matter to date has been unconscionable.

Therefore, should someone start to reform the courts? There was already some work done by the Australian Law Reform Commission regarding the Family Court of Australia, the FCA. Their recommendation was: abolish the FCA and merge it with the Federal Court. However, that idea seems to have died on the vine.

I hope you don't die of boredom while reading this chapter, as there is nothing more yawn-worthy than reading bureaucratese.

Recommendations presented by the Committee on Australia's judicial system include:
1) the High Court of Australia adopt a written complaint handling policy and make it publicly available; 2) no personal details of either the complainant or judicial officer be identifiable from these reports [I'm like Huh?]; 3) the process for appointments to the High Court should be principled and transparent;

4) the High Court of Australia Act 1969 prohibition on Federal judges holding another office of profit be retained;
5) the Commonwealth government establish a Federal judicial commission modeled on the Judicial Commission of New South Wales; and 6) within 12 months the government undertake planning and budgetary processes necessary for the establishing this commission. [See what I mean?]

Reuters studied the punishments of judges, 2008 to 2019: 1,509 judges in the US retired or were publicly disciplined following accusations of misconduct. In addition, in 3,613 cases, states disciplined wayward judges but kept hidden from the public key details of their offenses – including the identities of the judges.

"All told, 9 of every 10 judges were allowed to return to the bench after they were sanctioned for misconduct, Reuters determined. They included a California judge who had sex in his courthouse chambers, a New York judge who berated domestic violence victims; and a Maryland judge who, after his arrest for driving drunk, was allowed to return to the bench provided he took a Breathalyzer test before each appearance."]

Other cases: In Utah, a judge texted a video of a man's scrotum to court clerks. He was reprimanded but remains on the bench. In Indiana, three judges attending a conference last spring got drunk and sparked a 3 a.m. brawl outside a White Castle fast-food restaurant that ended with two of the judges shot.

Although the state supreme court found the three judges had "discredited the entire Indiana judiciary," each returned to the bench after a suspension.

"Per Curiam: We find the Respondents—the Honorable Andrew Adams, Judge of the Clark Circuit Court 1, the Honorable Bradley B. Jacobs, Judge of the Clark Circuit Court 2, and the Honorable Sabrina R. Bell, Judge of the Crawford Circuit Court—engaged in judicial misconduct by appearing in public in an intoxicated state ... and by becoming involved in a verbal altercation.

In Texas, a judge burst in on **jurors deliberating the case of a woman charged with sex trafficking** and declared that God told him the defendant was innocent.

In New York, a judge was reprimanded for having a bumper sticker on his car: "Boobies make me smile" and wearing a gun in the court parking lot when his permit was for concealed-carry only. He said he felt deep remorse.

Complaint Mechanism in New South Wales

The website judcom.nsw.gov.au tells us [Emphasis added]:

Complaints about New South Wales judicial officers

Please note the Judicial Commission is not a court. It has no power to overturn a court's decision. If you are unhappy with a court's decision you may wish to seek your own legal advice.

The Judicial Commission can only examine complaints about the ability and behaviour of current New South Wales judicial officers. A New South Wales judicial officer means: a magistrate; a judge of the District Court; a judge of the Supreme Court; a judge of the Land and Environment Court; the President of the Civil and Administrative Tribunal; and a Commissioner of the Industrial Relations Commission.

The Judicial Commission has no power to examine complaints against a retired New South Wales judicial officer, a tribunal member, a federal judicial officer, a legal practitioner, a court officer or a police officer.

The *Judicial Officers Act* 1986 provides a means for people to complain about the ability or behaviour of judicial officers (but not their decisions) and to have those complaints examined by an independent body. **Our complaint function is protective: we have no power to discipline judicial officers**, only to protect the public from judicial officers who are not fit for office or lack the capacity to discharge their duties. Our function is also to protect the judiciary from unwarranted intrusions into their judicial independence. The Commission cannot:

- provide legal advice or legal representation
- review a case for judicial error, mistake or other legal grounds
- discipline or sanction a judicial officer
- investigate allegations of criminal or corrupt conduct
- investigate a complaint about a retired judicial officer, federal judicial officer, arbitrator, assessor, registrar, member of a tribunal or legal practitioners.

South Australia has a Judicial Conduct Commissioner appointed under the *Judicial Conduct Commissioner Act 2015* (JCC Act). Its website, jcc.sa.gov.au, outlines the complaint process:

*Can I make a complaint? Yes, if you have not been declared a vexatious litigant.
*If you would like to make a public interest disclosure, please complete the hardcopy form, email it to admin@jcc.sa.gov.au. When we receive your complaint we will conduct a preliminary examination.... We might contact you to clarify issues ... the Commissioner decides how to deal with your complaint. If the Commissioner thinks there might be corruption they will refer your complaint to the Office for Public Integrity. [i.e., the graveyard]

If your complaint does not raise an issue of corruption, the Commissioner could refer your complaint to the relevant jurisdictional head [who] would be required to report back to the Commissioner advising the action taken [regarding] you complaint.

*Alternatively, the Commissioner could recommend that the Attorney-General appoint a judicial conduct panel to inquire into and report on the issues arising from your complaint. The Commissioner could only make that recommendation if he thought an inquiry into the conduct was necessary or justified and that if the conduct was established it may warrant consideration of removal of the judicial officer.

*In the most serious of cases, the Commissioner could make a report directly to Parliament.

*In some instances following a preliminary examination, no action will be taken. It might be that the Commissioner is obliged to dismiss your complaint in accordance with the *Judicial Conduct Commissioner Act 2015 (JCC Act)* or that he is satisfied that further consideration of your complaint would be unjustified.

The JCC Act contains strict confidentiality obligations [about] social media or publishing in the newspaper, television or radio. It is an offence to breach a prohibition on publication.

8. When Is a Suppression Order Justified?

(L) Gag order, Photo: dc.medill.northwestern.edu (R) Cling peaches, Photo: delightedcooking.com

Dr Pridgeon thinks he may end up doing the Jailhouse Rock for many years. Ergo, he needs your support. But something stands in the way of publicity for his case. Namely, the ability of judges to censor information. In principle, all criminal trials are open for us to gaze at. What do courts want to prevent us from seeing?

Early in 2023, a forthcoming trial was officially announced as "*The King v Patrick O'Dea, Russell Pridgeon and __ __*." The third name was printed; I, being intimidated have removed it. We had never run into this before, suppression of an already-announced name!

The secret name is that of the grandmother, whom Patrick assisted to get her grandson protected from an abuser. Her case got shunted off to join another, which I also dare not mention. Judge Leanne Clare has ordered it suppressed -- though it has for years been openly described on Internet *and* by mainstream media.

I've decided to refer to the grandmother's cases as Cling Peaches. Allow me to explain. In the sitcom, *All in the Family,* the husband, Archie Bunker, used to berate his wife, Edith. He ordered her to stop talking about cling peaches. So she had to say "Mm, mm-mm" when she needed to refer to them. It would be too inconvenient for me here to say *Mm, mm-mm,* so I'll say "Cling Peaches."

The previous chapters established that that courts engage in child stealing (on the pretext of a child's best interest) and that a courtroom is a place where magistrates can cause evidence to be hidden. Now let's see how gag orders and court closures may work.

Three laws in New South Wales are on point: the *Court Suppression and Non-publication Orders Act* 2010 (aka "the *Suppression Act*"), the *Criminal Procedure Act* 1986, and the *Children (Criminal Proceedings) Act* 1987. Plus, outside of statutory law, judges claim inherent power (under "contempt of court") to order suppression.

I begin with a letter that Pridgeon wrote, complaining that a tribunal had wrongly put a lid on a case in which he was defending himself, and then I'll quote from the very helpful "bench book."

I'll quote Pridgeon's letter to Court, objecting to the use of suppression orders, on grounds of open justice. Being unemployed from 2018 to 2022, Dr Pridgeon had spare time to write, such as:

"It was unclear on 1 March 2021 whether Medical Council lawyer Ms [Alexandra] Rose was signaling her intention to make application for (sec 91) Non-publication orders, or (sec 92) Suppression orders, prohibiting or restricting the disclosure of information.

"What is the intent of such orders? The intent of suppression/non-publication orders is the public interest. My first submission is that such orders will not add to this Tribunal's ability to perform its functions. It will be against public interest.... It appears motivated for the convenience and reputation of the institutions who have failed to protect these children, and the men who abused the children. It will hide the crimes against these children from public scrutiny. It is not going to help the children.

"What is the principle for exercise of this discretionary power? There is **no inherent power to exclude the public** from knowing what is going on in this case. The principle to guide discretionary decision is that **open justice is fundamental to justice**.

"Noting the Prime Minister's October 2018 apology to victims, parents and whistle-blowers, it highly relevant to the public interest issue to see how I, as a whistle-blower, will be dealt with.

"What will a suppression or non-publication order do? I was deeply angered but not surprised that Ms Rose advised she was going to ask that the Tribunal, using s 8(1)(c), considers whether "the order is necessary to protect the safety of any person." The only way the authorities will act to protect these children, is if they are forced to do so by public pressure. The better question is, cui bono? Who benefits by suppressing the details of this case as it exposes the children's abuse?

"I continue to be astounded that **Australians who work within Australian institutions continue to behave as if they are absolved of all moral and legal responsibility simply by the fact that they are performing their assigned tasks**. Hannah Arendt wrote about this extensively after she was assigned to cover the Trial of prominent Nazi Adolph Eichmann.

"Her book *Eichmann in Jerusalem* was notable for its *subtitle: A report on the Banality of Evil.* Eichmann claimed he bore no responsibility for the genocide that he had overseen, because he was simply "doing his job". Eichmann is quoted as saying "*He did his duty.*" "*He not only obeyed orders, he obeyed the law.*" "*He was unable to change anything*". Upon seeing members of "respectable society" endorsing mass murder, Eichmann felt that his moral responsibility was relaxed, as if he were Pontius Pilate.

"There is written law and unspoken law, such as the (often uncodified) law which evildoers sustain to enable their deeds: Eichmann, Hitler, and paedophiles in power have a 'law' that no-one 'dobs' and the names of the guilty are protected. ...

"With respect to Ms Rose's proposed suppression orders, it is completely absurd, to pretend to be concerned about the privacy of these children ...Is it possible do you think, that these children aren't coming to harm? ... National media has already published and linked the identities of the children. Everybody knows. This suppression order **raises concerns about bad faith.**

Yet the Tribunal members, His Honour Judge Le Poer Trench, Dr J. Aitken, Dr E. Summers and S. Lovrovich denied Russell's request that he **be allowed to openly discuss his defense.** They cited "s64(1)(c) of the Civil and Administrative Tribunal Act."

Now for the NSW judges' bench book, abridged but not altered, except I add bolding, and I comment in square brackets.

Closed court, suppression, and non-publication orders.
(1-349) **Introduction.** The onus is on the parties to make an application for appropriate orders at the hearing. Such orders may include an application for a pseudonym order or the suppression of certain evidence, such as evidence related to assistance given during the proceedings... (See *Sentencing Bench Book* at 12-202 Procedure to **reduce penalties for assistance to authorities**).

Common law and suppression and non-publication orders
The *Suppression Act* does not limit or otherwise affect any **inherent jurisdiction** a court has to regulate its proceedings or **deal with contempt of court**: s 4. The implied powers of a court are directed to preserving its ability to perform its functions in the administration of justice: *BUSB v* R (2011) per Spigelman CJ.

[I'll buy that idea, but only if it's deployed honestly.]

[1-350] The principle of open justice. [Fasten seatbelts, please!] The principle of open justice is a fundamental aspect of the system of justice in Australia and the **conduct of proceedings in public is an essential quality** of an Australian court of justice.

There is **no inherent power** of the court **to exclude the public:** *John Fairfax Publications Pty Ltd v District Court of NSW* (2004). However, in appropriate cases [says who?] courts have jurisdiction to modify and adapt the content of general rules of open justice and procedural fairness and to make non-publication orders for particular kinds of cases: *HT v The Queen* [2019].

[I hear that the court got closed in the Cling Peaches case. Why?]

Section 6 of the *Suppression Act* reflects the **legislative intention that orders under the Act should only be made in exceptional circumstances**.... In some cases, where reporting of particular proceedings is misleading, emotive and **encourages vigilante** behaviour, the message disseminated may be "antithetical to institutionalized justice" and a non-publication order may not compromise the public interest in open justice.... [Hmm.]

Although the parties may reach agreement as to appropriate redactions, the court must determine for itself whether the proposed redactions should be the subject of a suppression order, having regard to, in particular, the emphasis in sec 6 on the need to safeguard the public interest in open justice. [Son of a gun!]

The redacted judgment must remain intelligible, particularly as to the matters of principle justifying the decision to suppress. [Yay!]

Court Suppression and Non-publication Orders Act 2010
The *Suppression Act.* The power in s 7 is broad and may, depending on the particular circumstances, extend to a judicial officer in one court (for example, the District Court) making non-publication orders with the capacity **to affect proceedings in another.** [Some say the suppression in Cling Peaches is aimed at depriving Russell's trial of making relevant quotes from testimony.]

A "non-publication order" and a "suppression order" are defined in s 3. A "party" is broadly defined in s 3. Those persons entitled to be heard on an application are set out in s 9(2)(d) and include news media organizations. [Gumshoe can be equated to a party?]

Section 8(1) of the *Suppression Act* sets out the grounds upon which an order can be made. **Mere belief** that an order is necessary **is insufficient.** Nor is it enough that it appears to the Court that the proposed order is convenient, reasonable or sensible.

The expression "administration of justice" in s 8(1)(a) extends to the protection of confidential **police methods** as well as the investigation and detection of crime: *R v Elmir.*

Content of the order. An order *must* specify ... the grounds on which it was made: s 8(2). When information on the internet is involved, service providers must be identified and given the opportunity to remove relevant material before an order is sought. ... Orders made under the Act are subject to review and appeal....

9. Lawyers, Have You Seen Any of These Transgressions?

Photo: nswbar.asn.au

The railway tracks photo is from the Professional Conduct page of the New South Wales Bar Association' website, without a caption. I presume it means "Stay on the Straight and Narrow." This chapter presents selections from NSW Code for Barristers, 2015. That is a Rule, not a statute. Note: Both Russell Pridgeon and Patrick O'Dea reside in NSW -- no one sems to know why their case, which is federal, is being tried in Queensland. How's that for amazing.

"Legal Profession Uniform Conduct," aka Barristers Rules

... 4 Principles. These Rules are made in the belief that: (a) barristers owe their **paramount duty to the administration of justice,**
(b) barristers must maintain high standards of professional conduct, (c) barristers as specialist advocates in the administration of justice, **must act honestly, fairly, skillfully, bravely and with competence and diligence,**

5 Interpretation. The *Interpretation of Legislation Act 1984* (Victoria) applies to the interpretation of these Rules.

7 Other standards. These Rules are not intended to be a complete or detailed code of conduct for barristers. Other standards for ... are found in the inherent disciplinary jurisdiction of the Supreme Court, the legislation regulating the legal profession and in the general law (including the **law relating to contempt of court**).

Advocacy rules
8 General. **A barrister must not engage in conduct which is:**
(a) dishonest or otherwise discreditable to a barrister,

(b) prejudicial to the administration of justice, or
(c) likely to diminish public confidence in the legal profession [!!]

9 Another vocation. A barrister must not engage in another vocation [such as CIA? ASIO? Mafia?] which: (a) is liable to adversely affect the reputation of the legal profession or the barrister's own reputation, (b) **is likely to impair or conflict with the barrister's duties** to clients....

23 Duty to the court. A barrister has an overriding duty to the court to act with independence in the interests of the administration of justice. [Good heavens.]

24 A barrister must not deceive or knowingly or recklessly mislead the court. [Astonishing.]

25 A barrister must take all necessary steps to correct any mis- leading statement made by the barrister **to a court as soon as possible after the barrister becomes aware that the statement was misleading.** [When the saints come marching in...]

34 A barrister must inform the court of any apparent misapprehension by the court as to the effect of an order which the court is making, as soon as the barrister becomes aware of the misapprehension. [Has this ever been done? Show me a case.]

35 Duty to the client. A barrister must promote and protect fearlessly and by all proper and lawful means the client's best interests to the best of the barrister's skill and diligence, **and do so without regard to his or her own interest or to any consequences to the barrister or to any other person.** [Bullseye!]

39 Criminal pleas. It is the duty of a barrister representing a person charged with a criminal offence: (a) to advise the client generally about any plea to the charge, and (b) to make clear that the client has complete freedom of choosing the pleas to be entered.

42 Independence. A barrister must not act as a mere mouthpiece and must exercise the forensic judgments called for during the case independently, after appropriate consideration of the client's and the instructing solicitor's wishes.... [Show me a case.]

45 A barrister must not in the presence of any of the parties or solicitors **deal with a court on terms of informal personal familiarity** which may reasonably give the appearance that the barrister has special favour with the court. [Happens all the time.]

49 Duty to the opponent. A barrister must not knowingly make a false or misleading statement to an opponent in relation to the case (including its compromise). [*Incroyable.*]

50 A barrister must take all necessary steps to correct any false or misleading statement case made by the barrister to an opponent as soon as possible after the barrister becomes aware that the statement was false or misleading. [Ask Pridgeon about this.]

54 A barrister **must not**, outside an ex parte application or a hearing of which an opponent has had proper notice, **communicate in the opponent's absence with the court concerning** any matter of substance in connection with proceedings....

58 A barrister must seek to ensure that work which the barrister is briefed to do in relation to a case is done so as to:
(a) confine the case to identified issues genuinely in dispute **...**
(c) present the identified issues in dispute clearly and succinctly ....

60 Responsible use of court process and privilege A barrister must take care to ensure that the barrister's advice to invoke the coercive powers of a court: (b) is appropriate for the robust advancement of the client's case on its merits, **(c) is not given principally in order to harass or embarrass a person, and** (d) is not given principally in order to gain some collateral advantage for the client or the barrister or the instructing solicitor or a **third party....**

62 In proceedings in which an allegation of sexual assault, indecent assault or the commission of an act of indecency is made ...
(a) a barrister must not ask that witness a question ....which is intended: (i) to mislead or confuse the witness, or **(ii) to be unduly annoying, harassing, intimidating, offensive, oppressive, humiliating, or repetitive, and**
(b) a barrister must take into account any particular vulnerability of

the witness **in the manner and tone of the questions that the barrister asks.** [Did you ever dream that such a rule existed?]

63 A barrister does not infringe rule 62 merely because ... (b) the questioning requires the witness to give evidence that the witness could consider to be offensive, distasteful or private.

65 A barrister must not allege any matter of fact amounting to criminality, fraud or other serious misconduct against any person unless the barrister believes on reasonable grounds that: **(a) available material by which the allegation could be supported provides a proper basis for it.**

67 A barrister must not make a suggestion in cross-examination on credit unless the barrister believes on reasonable grounds that acceptance of the suggestion would diminish the credibility of the evidence of the witness. [Elementary, my dear Watson.]

74 A barrister must not take any step to prevent or discourage prospective witnesses from conferring with an opponent or being interviewed by ... any other person involved in the proceedings.

76 Media comment. A barrister must not publish or take any step towards the publication of any material concerning any proceeding which: (a) is known to the barrister to be inaccurate ...

77 A barrister must not take any step towards the publication of any material concerning any current proceeding in which the barrister is appearing ... other than: (a) a barrister may supply answers to unsolicited questions concerning a current proceeding provided that the answers are limited to information as to the identity of the parties or of any witness already called, the nature of the issues in the case, the nature of the orders made including any reasons given by the court and the client's intentions as to any further steps in the case, or

(b) a barrister may, where it is not contrary to legislation or court practice and at the request of the client or instructing solicitor or in response to unsolicited questions **supply for publication:** (i) **copies of pleadings in their current form** which have been filed and served in accordance with the court's requirements,

(ii) **copies of affidavits or witness statements**, which have been read, tendered or verified in open court, clearly marked so as to show any parts ... which have been disallowed on objection. (iv) copies of exhibits admitted in open court and without restriction on access.

78 A barrister: (a) may if requested advise a client about dealings with the media but not in a manner which is calculated to interfere with the proper administration of justice ... [Example?]

79 Delinquent or guilty client. A barrister who... is informed ... that the client or a witness...: **(a) has lied in a material particular to the court or has procured another person to lie to the court ...** (c) has suppressed or procured another person to suppress material evidence upon a topic where there was a positive duty to make disclosure to the court, **must refuse to take any further part in the case** unless the client authorises the barrister to inform the court of the lie ... [Bring me my smelling salts, please.]

83 Prosecutor's duties. A prosecutor must fairly assist the court to arrive at the truth. [I can't handle this.]

85 A prosecutor must not, by language or other conduct, **seek to inflame or bias the court against the accused.** [Seriously?]

92 A prosecutor must not confer with or interview any accused except in the presence of the accused's legal representative. [Ask Martin Bryant. But that was TAS, not NSW.]

PROFESSIONAL CONDUCT The Bar Association's Professional Conduct Department facilitates the investigation and reporting to Bar Council of **conduct complaints** referred to the Bar Council by the Office of the Legal Services Commissioner.

Note: If that last one is like BBO -- the Massachusetts Board of Bar Overseers -- all made up of judges, you can forget about them kicking another judge out. Oh wait. Maybe if they saw a good judge they would have to do what must be done.

Wish I were joking here -- MM

10. Can the Legal Profession Survive in Its Current State?

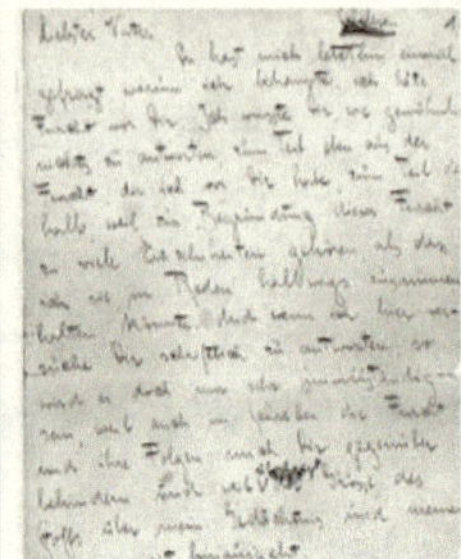

(L) Protestor dressed as Gitmo prisoner at Law School Graduation, Photo: sfgate.com (C) Kafka's letter to his father (R) Officer Pat Allen, Facebook

Just before graduating from University of Adelaide Law School in 2011, I enrolled for the GDLP, Graduate Diploma in Legal Practice. The lady at the Law Society handed each of us a list of local psychologists whom we might consult, as "new lawyers tend to get depressed." I don't think the Law Society tried to discern the cause of depression but, thinking about it now, it seems clear.

This chapter lists negative influences on the law profession. As we will see in Chapter 13, attorney Wilfred Seymour was happy to serve the world by making the law work well. That is not possible now. Courts in their current state do not serve the world.

1. The first negative influence on lawyers that we should list is simply the **increase in lawlessness**. Folks don't jump to the sound of a law being read out. They are more likely to roll their eyes. It is assumed that 'virtue' is outdated. I chalk this up to the free-rider problem. If a very small number of people on the train don't pay the fare, that's OK. But if the number becomes substantial, those who pay feel like fools. When the client comes into your law office, he might ask you how he can jump the turnstile.

2. Justice warriors must calculate the likelihood of **SLAPP**, i.e., a Strategic Lawsuit against Public Participation. This is also known as having a powerful opponent deep-pocket you by keeping your lawsuit running until you are impoverished or exhausted. As soon as the lapp phenomenon was identified, it should have been dealt with by judges. They have power to stop it, but they don't do so.

3. Judges are **not interested in justice**. How could they be? They all know of trials where the wrong man is convicted, such as Martin Bryant's case in 1996, but they do not discuss it. I suppose some judges are just plain scared but others "go along" with it.

4. Speaking of Martin Bryant, there is a whole apparatus of **criminal cops**. Other cops rarely complain. Pat Allen, pictured above, is an exception. He knows the truth about the Port Arthur case, in which he was told to stand down. There are many stand-downs.

5. The opposite is also true: cops **(or more likely mercenaries dressed as cops)** are sent in to commit the actual crime for which your client is blamed. Can you take them on?

6. If you are defending an accused, look at the **conflict of interest** of the other side. Rules for Prosecutors tell prosecutors to cough up any exculpatory evidence (in US, "Brady material"). But their loyalty is to the police who arrested your client. The prosecutor wants to win. And he expects a judge to side with the prosecution.

7. Maybe some of the players are in a **secret society**. In his book *The Rape of Justice*, Eustace Mullins shows how an accused, or a plaintiff or defendant in a lawsuit, can signal the judge that he is a Freemason by performing a gesture known as "the widow's son." Cops are heavily invested in Masonry. The deck is stacked!

8. Judges have **too much discretion**. In a world where they do not have a feel for the glories of the law, or are compromised, they can use these "inherent powers" to up-end justice. For example, Judge Leanne Clare, in an Operation Noetic case, has used powers of closing the court and suppressing names in such a way as to sever the accused from their supporters. It is possible for parliament to curtail that to some extent by legislation, and it's also possible to hold judges to account for crimes against justice.

9. Folks are **loathe to trust a lawyer** to work for them, as the cultural expectation is that she will only pursue their case according to her own interests, such as to lengthen the case to get more billing or to please a judge whom she has a need to please.

10. How Do You Think Lawyer Jokes Got That Way?

* A law-office receptionist took a call from a man asking to speak to Mr. Carlson. "I'm sorry, sir," the receptionist said, "he recently passed away." "Oh, is that right? Goodbye." But every day for a week the same man called back with the same question. Finally, the receptionist said, "Sir, why do you keep phoning for Mr Carlson after I've told you that he died?" "Oh, I just like to hear it."

* Man walks into a pub carrying his pet alligator, and asks the barman "Do you serve lawyers here?" "We sure do," says the barman. "Then I'll have a beer and give me a lawyer for my alligator."

* Q. What did the businessman advise his son?
A. Don't ever go to a lawyer without seeing a lawyer first.

* Q. What looks good on a lawyer, and is brown and black in color? A. A Doberman pinscher.

* Q. How can you stop a lawyer from drowning?
A. Just shoot him before he hits the water.

And there are more.

But I haven't yet touched the real reason for law student to get depressed during their first week on the job. It is that what they learned in law school belongs to a confident system of reality, yet that reality has disappeared. There is utter fakery out there.

Look back to Chapter 5's Family Law section 70NAE ruling. The mother's behavior was just fine. Her reading of her three children was clearly correct -- they were abused by the father. And she had all she needed, in black-letter law, to win them back. Namely, she had a reasonable belief. In fact she had doctor's reports and kids' disclosures galore. But the judge did a "contortionist's delight" to show that the mother was wrong. I suspect the judge is connected to a child trafficking system. I note that she belongs to the IBA, International Bar Association, in which she is a member of the -- wait for it -- Judicial Conduct Committee.

Ah, but I mean to go even deeper than looking at the child-trafficking industry. There is the whole running of the professions by outside forces. Everybody knows how Big Pharma runs doctors and hospitals. During the pandemic, legislators were prodded to arrange a payment of $39,000 to 'providers,' for each person who was put on a ventilator (and nearly all of them died).

As for the individual doctors and nurses carrying out the ventilator nonsense, they feared losing their job. As Professor Philip Allott has pointed out, we are all trapped in one big economic system. So we can now expect the powerful to offer us even weirder things, such as transhumanism, and we have nowhere to run.

Wait! Hold it! That's giving up too soon. Philip Allott calls it false fatalism. I call it the worship of trends. It seems to me that the human brain easily adjusts to any behavior that looks like taking over. Already people say we will have complete surveillance, complete censorship, and other things that were always anathema.

Guess what. Love of the law could be a new trend. It could grow which is what trends do. For the moment, hear me out as regards "dealing with" the criminals. One might start with a "show cause" notice, as sent when a man does not pay child support, despite a court order that obliges him to do so. Here is a make-believe case:

Mr Peter Smth, You are hereby ordered to appear in my court at 55 Center St, Belltown, Utah, on Monday, 12 December 2021 at 11:00am, and show cause why you should not be held in contempt of court for failure to pay child support in October and November, as I ordered, for your son Barry.

Failure to appear as ordered may result in the issuance of a bench warrant for your immediate arrest, and in garnishment of your wages to the amount due for the two month's child support. You have the right to be represented by an attorney. Failure to appear is a further act of contempt for which the penalty is $400.00 and up to six months in prison.

-- Judge Pierre Lamoureaux, November 20, 2021

Based on that simple example, I now devise another Show Cause letter to a judge. I don't have a court from which to send it, but I'll pretend I do. Pseudonyms will be used, out of respect.

To: Judge Leo P Kelshaw,

You are hereby ordered to appear in Western Australia Supreme Court on Thursday, 11 August 2023, in Perth WA, to show cause why you should not be held in contempt for mocking the courts of this state by your *ex cathedra* words and actions in 2023.

Your five apparently contemptuous-of-court actions are:

1. When Dr Metzer tried to tell you, as the judge managing his case, that evidence was being hidden, you threatened him with criminal defamation and did not try to obtain the data he offered.

2. Where Mrs Jones needed the public to witness her trial, to counteract the lies told by the media, you closed the court.

3. You refused to let an intellectually handicapped woman, Ms Smith, have a McKenzie friend sit with her as she gave witness.

4. When a decision was made in court to drop certain charges and offer a substantially new charge against Mrs Zee, this required a new consent from the CDPP. But none was sought. Thus, Mrs Zee, as a self-represented person, had no time to prepare a new defense against this new charge, a great violation of due process.

5. In a court case, which was attended by media, you criticized the behavior of a solicitor unrelated to the case, causing him, TD, to receive public opprobrium and be disciplined by the profession.

Please bring with you any records you have that refute these criticisms of your actions or words. I hope the charges are incorrect.

Failure to attend will result in a contempt-of-court citation by me.

-- Chief Justice Norton Schalacter, Jr [Reader, this is fictional]

But that's not all. We now ask whether the sentence should be custodial. That is, should the contemnor go to jail rather than get a suspended sentence or pay a fine. Here, Magistrate Kelshaw has only been sent a 'show cause'; he may have an excellent cause to show, but for simplicity we will assume he does not offer one.

The signer of the letter, a Chief Justice, has somehow discovered Kelshaw's misdeeds. The Magistrate's contempt was broad; he let us all down by not giving due process to the Defendant. I believe he did more; he committed Blackstonian crimes. So, should he be incarcerated? I quote the NSW judges sentencing bench book:

Crimes (Sentencing Procedure) Act 1999, Section 3A "...to prevent crime by deterring ...other persons from committing similar offences"; and s 3A(f) "**to denounce** the conduct of the offender".

Court of Criminal Appeal has consistently held that offences against justice require strong deterrent sentences and must be **severely** punished whenever detected: *Marinellis v* R [2007].

...It is accepted that an **offender's status as a senior legal practitioner and former judge** rendered perjury and perverting the course of justice more serious.... *Einfeld v* R.

Div 2 *Crimes Act* 1900, sec 314 "A person who makes an accusation intending a person to be the subject of an investigation of an offence, **knowing that other person to be innocent** of the offence, is liable to imprisonment for 7 years." [Sound familiar?]

In R *v Nomchong*, McInerney J ... endorsed the trial judge's reasoning that "... the inevitable consequence of the conviction of a **police officer for the offence of attempting to pervert the course of justice** would in most cases be a **custodial** sentence".

Section 323(a) provides a maximum penalty of **seven years** for intending to cause a witness in any judicial proceeding to withhold true evidence... it strikes at the integrity of the justice system and so some form of custodial sentence is normally appropriate: *Warby v* R [2007] ... *Asplund v* R *(Cth)* [2014].

End of Part Two: Law //   A Poem: "If, for Doctors"

in the style of Rudyard Kipling, written by Mary Maxwell a few years ago, as a comment at ageofautism.com

If you should learn who gave us this Vaccine Court,
And realize your participation in a crime,
If you can wonder how it be sport
For more babies to be allowed to lose their mind,

If you can hear that Pasteur was a cheat,
And know that Edward Jenner hoaxed us all,
Start to see two centuries of science in defeat,
And determine to ask for a complete recall,

If you can endure remarks that other men may send you
And not turn back, but keep a forward gaze
And be the kind of friend you
Would wish for, with or without "professional" praise,

To end this tragedy before it brings more terror,
To help society put dishonesty on the wane,
And turn around colossal error,
No matter whose the loss, or whose the gain,

Then the families will transmit a grateful roar,
And joy will swiftly break out 'round the earth,
Truth'll make a good old court appearance, and what's more,
The title "Doctor" will resume its former worth.

Note: Here is a verse from Kipling's original poem *If,* suitable for O'Dea and Pridgeon:

> "If you can force your heart and nerve and sinew
> To serve your turn long after they are gone,
> And so hold on when there is nothing in you
> Except the will which says to them: 'Hold on!' ...."

(L) Patrick O'Dea (R) Ms Kathleen O'Dea, at Number 10, accompanied by Shadow Foreign Sec'y Michael Ancram, left, and Euro MP Neil Parish, Photo: Richard Austin, Western Morning News.

During this vigil of the Brisbane trial of Pridgeon and O'Dea, I've hardly known anything about Patrick. So I typed "O'Dea, Zimbabwe" into a search and what came up was Patrick's sister Kathleen O'Dea. Her marvelous autobiography is called "Marshmallow Fishes." I ordered it from abebooks.com, and now it is in my hand. It's also in my spirit — eegads what a book!

It was published in 2014, so it's not about Operation Noetic. It's about joy. It's about being alive. It's about caring for the people in one's nation. Let me ask you — offhand — how many times have you knocked on the door of 10 Downing Street to recommend prime ministerial action? I'll bet not too many. But Kathleen (b 1964) couldn't help herself. She was driven to help Zimbabwe. She knocked. (She was trying to get Tony Blair to intervene for the tortured and starving people in Zimbabwe.)

Boy, trauma is not a nice thing — imagine having to experience it every day, on and on! In her book, Kathleen admits to having never got over watching people be killed or tortured when Mugabe's troops were fighting "the enemy" (i.e., whites, but also hundreds of thousands of blacks). I originally planned to recount, from Kathleen's book, some scenes of the Bush War, in which her older bro, Patrick O'Dea (and also Russell Pridgeon) were soldiers. But instead I will show you happy scenes. I urge you to buy the book as it's a real page-turner — describing her life in Africa, England, and now Australia.

And yes, I am trying to show where Patrick hails from. Kathleen herself is a justice warrior. Let us remember that the thing for which Patrick has now been suffering for 1,675 days (as of May 22, 2023), is The Law coming down on a man who was doing justice-warrior work, trying to protect a helpless boy. Got that?

Today, I switch from my "Let's arrest the judges" mode to my "Please give this man mercy" mode. It's not for me to say that Patrick has had actual terror for 1,675 days. I've never met him. But he already had painful war wounds (in the spine).

So wouldn't it be nice if Australia could stand up for him and say "Give this guy a break." Hmm, his lawyer might not appreciate that, if it interferes with strategy. Oh wait, he ain't got no lawyer. Still, I'm taking a risk here. The author of *Marshmallow Fishes*, Kathleen O'Dea, allows me to quote 7 pages from Chapter 1 of her work. So sit back and enjoy. If you can't read it now, come back to it later. It is so energizing! Kath was national champ of backstroke in 1979 in Rhodesia. She came to Australia at age 21 and later played on the Australian team of underwater hockey!

Chapter One, of *Marshmallow Fishes*

I WAS born in Bulawayo. My dad was Scottish. He had emigrated to Rhodesia when he was in his early 20's. He had a choice. It was Rhodesia or Alaska. *(Shit! I could have been an Eskimo!)* My dad, John McGarry O'Dea, was born in Glasgow in 1926. My mom, Daphne Lena Ferreira, was born in Gwelo, Rhodesia in 1927. Her dad was of Portuguese origin. The name of Gwelo was changed to Gweru when Mugabe came to power. Just like he changed Salisbury to Harare, he changed the names of all roads in Bulawayo. Overnight, Matabele names or English names became Shona names.

Before all that happened Mr and Mrs O'Dea happily reared four kids. Patrick, Sharon, Theresa and me. Their first born was named Patrick I was the last, born prematurely.

All the girls went to convent school and Patrick went to Christian Brothers College. I started swimming before I was five. We lived in the poorer part of town then, North End. Living in those poorer places never affected us. We would look up to the kids who had nicer things but we never felt deprived.

I used to collect all the stray dogs. One was a black bitsa dog (*bitsa this and bitsa that!*) that we used to call *Blackballs*. He would go wandering and bailing him out of the pound became an expensive pastime. My dad soon discovered that it was cheaper if he pretended he wanted to give a home to a pet, rather than to own up and say *Blackballs* already was our pet, but it was a dead giveaway when *Blackballs* always went nuts when he saw my dad. I think the guys at the pound eventually turned a blind eye.

My dad worked for Rhodesian Railways as a train driver. He would do the Mafeking run into Botswana. Often he would come home with one of the huge tortoises they would find on the side of the railway tracks. My mom was a typist. She was secretary to Brigadier Shaw who was later killed in a helicopter crash. It must have been pressurised work because everything was top secret. We were fighting a war. Even as a child I could not understand how that big wide world out there could let this happen.

Our favourite treat was marshmallow fishes. If we didn't have any money we would hang around the tuck shop and cling to the bars looking pleadingly at the African shop keeper, who was called Jock, hoping that we might get a marshmallow fish for free. He would often swing a couple of free fishes our way.

As a kid those marshmallow fishes made such an impact. It is funny how something like that meant so much to us kids. Sometimes you got to notice that your fish was missing an eye (*perhaps the mould didn't always work properly*) and I would feel sorry for that fish. Before I ate a marshmallow fish I would have to make the huge decision to chomp the tail first or the head. I always felt guilty if I ate the head first.

[MM — See what we're dealing with here?]

Somehow, marshmallow fishes seem to stand for the uncomplicated innocence of our lives in Rhodesia before so much shit hit the fan and changed our lives and our land for ever. Marshmallow fishes were childhood expectation; our hope and happiness.

All of us O'Dea kids could swim. We were naturals. We all swam competitively and we were always making the headlines. Patrick and Sharon both captaining our province Matabeleland. Sharon then went on from competitive swimming to synchronised swimming for Rhodesia.

The Way We Were. O'Deas, L to R: Theresa, 7, Sharon, 14, dad John, mum Daphne, Patrick, 15, Kathleen, 6 on Patrick's lap.

Patrick went to Christian Brothers College. He was naughty, so the Catholic brothers refused to award him with his sports colours blazer. So to piss everyone off he managed to get his name on the college cups for swimming and athletics and made the first eleven at cricket and the first fifteen at Rugby. But still they never gave him his sports blazer. Perhaps that's why he's such a grump arse. I'm only teasing. I love Patrick to bits.

Ted Broster was my coach and he could see my potential, although it took a bit of coaxing. Getting to that stage, I must have quit about twenty times, so it became a joke. My dad would say: *"So, Kathleen. Are you retiring this week?"* I was about 8 years old. My dad would be one of the judges in competitions and one time he disqualified Theresa. Some of the over pushy parents could not believe it: *"He's disqualified his own daughter!"* they said. I loved my dad. He had good values.

We kept making the newspapers as swimmers so being poor didn't really bother us. Looking back now, I can see that we had status in other ways. Not that I am one for status or material things. I am more concerned about justice.

I remember one of my bosses in Australia, John Brown an ex-air force man, saying to me: *"Kathleen, how did you ever swim?"* I said: *"Why?"* He said: *"You never look left or right."* He was being deep. He meant in life, because if I sense injustice in anything I don't mess about. I just put my blinkers on and go for it because I have to try and stop it.

We were taught by Dominican nuns. They were quite harsh. Most of them were German. I am sure I was supposed to be left handed but I was made to write right-handed. If I didn't, I would get a rap on the knuckles with a wooden ruler.

A psychologist who helped me with post-traumatic stress told me: *"Kathleen, you are so determined to make the world the way you want it to be. It is just not going to happen."* Well one day it might.

We used to share the swimming pool with boys from the Milton School but I never had much to do with boys. Boys and girls would admire each other from afar. Just a look was all it took. You could be boyfriend and girlfriend without even talking to each other! My childhood sweetheart was Harry and my friend Tracy's was Guy. Many years later we all met up again in Perth, Australia, Harry and I just friends, Tracy and Guy now married. Guy and Harry were complaining that they had had to leave Zimbabwe and go to Australia to lose their virginity!

In 1974 my brother Patrick joined the Army. I was about 10 years old. Patrick was 19. I really feared for him because there was so much death in this Rhodesian bush war that was being fought. When they were out on patrol my brother and his mate Jimmy Jeans would sit at the back of the army truck on the rear wheels because if they hit a landmine that would absorb a lot of the blast. One time when they hit a landmine my brother had the machine gun between his legs facing outwards on a sandbag. It was a MAG. Jimmy had a standard FN rifle. The normal procedure if you hit a landmine was to empty your magazine into the surrounding bush in case of an ambush.

After the huge shock of the blast Jimmy felt a tremendous weight on top of his head. Patrick's machine gun had been blown into the air and landed on his head.... Jimmy jokes that he is sure to this day that Patrick wanted either his girlfriend or his motor bike and saw an opportunity to take him out!

When the nights were very cold Jimmy used to wear ballet tights under his uniform trousers because that kept him warm. Patrick asked Jimmy to get him a pair as well. Unfortunately they had run out of black ones *(at least that's what Jimmy claimed)* so he bought Patrick a pair of pink ones. It then became a great prank for Patrick, wearing nothing but his pink ballet tights, to streak past the Major's tent. Another story they told was when there was a parade the main Army dude stuck his stick up the nose of one of the soldiers and shouted: *"What is this piece of shit on the end of this stick?"* The soldier's reply: *"It depends which end of the stick you are looking at, Sir!"*

So, all of this was going on while we were counting the tiles at the bottom of the swimming pool. School started at 7am but we would get up at 4.30am to go training first. We would complete 4,000 to 5,000 metres before school. If I remember correctly, we would do 4,000 metres in about an hour. Boy, did we smell of chlorine! What we were doing at that age would have been hailed as phenomenal in the first world countries. But it was just normal to us; we didn't know any different. My dad was so good. He would get up that early and cook breakfast for us at the pool.

My dad was so inspirational and intelligent and knowledgeable. You would never believe he was just a miner's son who left school at 14. He had such a wide perspective on life. If Mormons or Jehovah's Witnesses knocked on our door he would always invite them in and they would walk away knowing more about their own religion than when they walked in!

My dad was also a volunteer with the Good Samaritans, taking telephone calls from people whose lives were in desperate crisis, suicidal often. We were a bit backward in Rhodesia. It was that time warp thing I told you about, the world moving forward while we were fighting a war.

We loved our pets. We had *Nero*, a Bull Mastif cross; *Lady*, a Pekinese cross; *King*, a Great Dane; two miniature Fox Terriers, *Ben* and *Shelley* and two cats, *Buffy*, who was ginger and *Rubbish*, who Patrick named. My closest friend at high school was Debbie. We were inseparable. I was also close friends with Tracy and Shareen. Our paths have since crossed several times. Like me, they are travelling Zimbabweans. Their souls don't rest, either. Debbie married a farmer who was badly affected by everything Mugabe put us through.

Carol was great. She was a feisty, outspoken short girl who had wild uncontrollable hair. We used to have to wear our school hats in assembly but, because of Carol's wild locks, her boater could never sit properly on her head. This would irritate the teachers who would berate her for being scruffy. This was so unfair and it wasn't long before Carol had had enough of it. One day when we were all in assembly and the prefects were giving her a hard time she bellowed in her loudest voice, which was *very* loud: *"You think I **chose** to be born with this hair? Just because you have a piece of f****** tin on your tit it doesn't mean you can tell **me** what to do."*

Well said, Carol. That told 'em! If we'd been as gutsy as she was we would all have burst into a round of applause for her. Anyway, inside our heads, that's just what we were doing. Another time, when Carol was a bit late getting to school, a teacher asked her: *"Why are you so late?"* Carol said: "*Because you started before I got here."* I loved Carol. She had such spirit.

Our house in Catherine Berry Drive was just a few doors down from a Mess called Tarino Tavern-- a Mess was a rented house shared by young professional people. They had servants. We did, too. That was the way in Africa And for anybody who wants to pass judgement on that, listen: **We cared for them, heart and soul.** I have done the same sort of work myself in a first world country and I can promise you, **our** servants had the better deal.

The parties were many; too many, perhaps. But it was all just innocent fun. It was a way of coming together and having a normal life after the war, especially for those who were ex-Army. There was total unity between all the Mess dwellers; never any trouble or fights despite the booze. The good part was we did not have to worry about First Aid because we had a house full of doctors and vets.

One time *Fuzzy* and Geoff had had a few too many and *Fuzzy* had cut his forehead open on his beer glass and in both their states Geoff sewed him up with just an ordinary needle and thread and whatever alcohol was available to kill the germs.

It was beautifully done, hardly a scar. Just as talented were the vets in our midst like Johnny. The sort of conversation you would hear in the bar: "It's a bit different putting a dog under anaesthetic or prescribing penicillin and having to go and sort out a sick Ostrich. And how much anaesthetic do you give a Rhino?" [MM- now there's a serious question for you!]

The girls were Jayne, Tina, Deidre who had lost 14 of their family, killed in the Rhodesian war. Deidre's sister was in one of the Viscounts that were shot down by Nkomo. Then in February 1979 another missile attack brought down a second Air Rhodesia plane on the same flight. This time there were no survivors. All 59 died. Can you believe, that apart from the International Airline Pilots Association, there was no official condemnation of these outrages from anywhere? UK and US stayed silent as, some reckoned, they did not want to appear to be supporting Ian Smith.

They were a crazy bunch. But their skills were unbelievable; men like Barney, a chopper pilot who worked tirelessly and courageously to stop rhino horn poaching. Barney was so brave. Rhino horn poaching was for big rich pickings and the poachers were brutal killers of men as well as animals.

Mugabe's police and soldiers would just turn up at your house with AK47s to do searches for petrol and uniforms that would identify those who fought in the Bush wars. Just before I moved out of home my mom was lying in bed one morning. From her bed you could see straight down the passage onto our veranda and she saw about twelve police and soldiers, all armed with AK47s.

Mom was petrified. She had to let them into our garage so they could search it. I trailed behind and my heart was pounding. In the corner, a pair of my brother's Army boots was hanging from the beams. They didn't spot them, thank God, but it was a very close call.

[MM -- Very good. Patrick O'Dea remains alive, but the last four years of judicial torture, or 'Noetic' torture, have almost killed him. Even the Good Samaritan in the Bible didn't get clobbered for helping a helpless person, did he?

To repeat, Kath O'Dea did not write *Marshmallow Fishes* to help her brother. It's been in print since 2014. ... Buy a copy and have fun. Oh, it isn't all fun. Much of it is gory.]

12. The Solidarity of Doctors and a Lonely Yachtsman

A yacht in Freemantle, WA, Photo: AFP (cop pixelated)

Dr William Russell Pridgeon, a GP in Grafton NSW, is a graduate of the University of Cape Town, South Africa. He soon faces trial, We all need to be there, at least in spirit.

I now demand that ALL DOCTORS IN AUSTRALIA BE THERE, at least in spirit. Come on, you guys and gals, this is your moment. There is not a scintilla of evidence that Russell harmed anyone and in fact, he went way out of his way to help two children. The expert on child abuse, Prof Freda Briggs of the University of South Australia, had asked the good doctor to help, in 2014. He knew it was risky but he couldn't say No.

Anyway, Pridgeon went to the police and told them what was happening. So they can't say they needed to hunt for him (though' they do say so — after all, scripted drama is scripted drama.)

I can remember when doctors were looked up to by the community and were expected to help society when appropriate. Oh, is this, technically, part of their job? Well, yes. Doctors have such a high opinion of themselves that they incorporated that responsibility into the Code of Ethics. The following is the Australian Medical Association's code. I have cherry picked the items that bear on Russell's case:

AMA Code of Ethics 2004. Revised 2016

Members are advised of the importance of seeking the advice of colleagues should they be facing difficult ethical situations.

1. **PREAMBLE**

… 1.6 While doctors have a primary duty to individual patients, they also have responsibilities to other patients and the wider community.

1.7 The principles in the AMA *Code of Ethics* apply to all doctors regardless of their professional roles.

2. **Teaching**

2.6.1 *Honour your obligation* to pass on your professional knowledge and skills to colleagues and students, where appropriate.

3.1 Professional conduct

3.1.2 Build a professional reputation *based on integrity and ability.*

3.1.7 Accept responsibility for maintaining and improving the standards of the profession.

3.2 Working with colleagues

3.2.1 Treat your colleagues with respect and dignity.

4.1 Responsibility to society

4.2.3 Recognise your right to refuse to carry out services which you consider to be professionally unethical, against your moral convictions, imposed on you for either administrative reasons or for financial gain or which you consider are not in the best interests of the patient.

4.2.4 Alert appropriate authorities when the health care service or environment within which you work is inadequate or poses a threat to health.

4.2.5 The doctor who reasonably believes that significant harm will occur to the public as a result of the delivery or non-delivery of health care, despite the process mentioned in 4.2.4, would be open to taking whistleblowing action. **Contemporary protections for whistleblowers should be supported by doctors.** [Ahem!]

4.3 Health standards, quality and safety

4.3.2 Accept a share of the profession's responsibility to society in matters relating to the health and safety of the public, health education and literacy and legislation affecting the health of the community.

4.5 Medico-legal responsibilities

4.5.1 Recognise your responsibility when preparing medico-legal documents such as medical certificates or independent medical assessments. The information you provide must be honest, accurate and not misleading.

4.5.2 Recognise your responsibility to assist the courts, tribunals (or similar forums) by providing informed, fair opinion based on impartial, expert evidence when reasonably called upon to do so. [End of Excerpts from AMA Code of Ethics]

Today we need today. Unity. Togetherness. Professional responsibility. Moral standards. The (Aussie) AMA says so!

Quite possibly, the graduates of medical schools after 1990, or so, did not get the excellent brow-beating about their responsibilities that the older doctors got in medical school. After George, my physician-husband, passed away, one of his Adelaide students told me "When we saw Prof Maxwell, we broke out into a cold sweat." I am sure there were professors at Edinburgh who scared the hell out of George -- and he was always grateful for it.

Below, in Chapter 22, I discuss Australian Broadcasting Corps' persecution of Dr Bill McBride of Sydney. When he, in 1960, made the discovery that it was thalidomide that was causing children to be born with short limbs, he was feted and given awards. Later, when he whistleblew another matter, he was persecuted.

Happily one -- but only one -- doctor came to court to stand up for McBride: Dr Doulas Keeping, an obstetrician in Queensland, an Aberdonian. I later saw, in 2019, that upon Keeping's retirement, his patients sent wildly enthusiastic testimonials. This one takes the cake:

"You know when the midwives fight over who gets to work with Doug that he's a wonderful craftsman. He delivered me 35 years ago in a difficult vbac for my Mum. Then he delivered my two 9 pound 5, and 10 pound 1, vaginally. If having babies was easier and cheaper, I would have kept doing it just to see him! He deserves all the accolade and awards possible."

Note: On 30 May 2018, Dr Pridgeon wrote to the Minister of Child Safety in Queensland [Di Farmer] advising her that:

..."when I was able find safe accommodation for them I sheltered them in a safe house in my locality from about Easter 2014 for more than a year.

"This was one of the greatest privileges of my life to be able to help these children escape the horrific abuse inflicted upon them by fiends, and enabled by Rogue Judges, lawyers and Policemen who actively hid the truth, ignored evidence, and facilitated child rape, effectively trafficking these children to paedophiles.**"**

That was 5 months before the dramatic swoop-down arrest. Now I've found another writing by Russell which is so lovely you've got to hear it. Has a sad ending but so what.

Recall that the AFP said Dr Pridgeon was part of a syndicate and that he was **getting his yacht ready** to abduct children to New Zealand or Zimbabwe. As syndicates, do, I suppose. (My friend the late Trish Fotheringham, at age 12, was forced to help an actual syndicate lure children onto a boat near Vancouver, Canada.)

So now sit back and listen to the factaroonies: Why the yacht was in Perth, why Russell had one at all, and where he was planning to take it. Ah, facts! Remember facts?

The Yacht. By Russell Pridgeon

"The 'Courier Mail' told its readers the yacht was to be used to transport abducted children from Freemantle to Tasmania and then on to New Zealand or South Africa.

"So let me state the facts regarding the yacht: After being in Grafton for 18 years I realised that I had not had a serious holiday while I had been there. I was tired to my soul and longed for a break. After talking to a friend, my ambition to sail around the world was reawakened and as retirement was approaching, I determined to get a yacht again.

"I've always been interested in sailing. As a 12-year-old I built a sailing boat from plans from *Popular Mechanics.* [Shite!] I learned to sail on Matopos Dam, in a friend's Enterprise dinghy. Later I sailed Fireballs. At university I sailed Hobie-16's on False Bay Cape Town, and Lasers.

In my final year at medical school, I bought a Windsurfer and sailed on lakes and the sea and crewed on keelboats sailing out of the Royal Cape Yacht Club. Friends had 'Muira's' and 'Peterson 33's' and I helped one of them fix his 'Colin Archer' yacht up for a trip to Europe.

I developed a passion for the idea of sailing around the world and looked at the possibility of building my own yacht to do this. As a junior doctor I saved my salary and laid down the hull and deck of a H30 design by L Francis Herreshof, into which I poured my salary during the hyperinflation of the early 1980s in South Africa.

Inflation increased faster than I could earn the money to build the boat, and eventually after 6-7 years of boat building, completing the yacht slipped out of reach and I gave up on the idea when I decided to move to NZ.

"I was badly burned by the experience in South Africa and intense work pressure forced me to put my yacht-dream on hold while I lived and worked in NZ and then Australia. I however chartered catamarans in the Whitsundays for two holidays and enjoyed trying to relearn what I had forgotten.

"I was captivated by the 'Hans Christian 36', a very seaworthy design, and one was for sale in Freemantle. It required a lot of work to do all the deferred maintenance.

So I bought a very run-down boat that I fixed up, and actually really enjoyed doing it. I also did Radio and Sailing exams and practical RYA courses while I was there. A dear relative flew to join me, and we did a RYA sailing course together. I replaced the standing rigging, the sails and fitted a 'Cap Horn' wind vane. There was a huge amount of work.

"A very old friend asked if he could join me on my proposed trip back to the East coast. I planned to sail into the Southern Ocean and pass south of Tasmania, before travelling north to NSW. It would have been an epic trip, and not for the faint-hearted. I didn't realise how ill he was and was relieved when he pulled out.

Shortly before I was due to head out, I discovered I did not have enough power in my left hand to pull down the sails – the hand was weakened from a nasty wrist fracture a few years previously.

"Insofar as refitting the yacht, I had always wanted to do a circumnavigation around Australia. My ambition remains to sail the four Capes. I suppose I wanted to do what my great-grandfather had done when he sailed around Cape Horn, and of course as a youngster I was inspired by Francis Chichester's exploits and the books by Bernard Moitessier and David Lewis.

"Once I was arrested, on strict bail, I was prohibited from leaving NSW and unable to get to Fremantle to care for the boat. I then had to sell the boat to pay legal fees and to avoid the ongoing marina fees.

Sadly, I had no option but to leave my dream behind. Selling the yacht was a real wrench, the loss of a lifelong dream, a lot of invested money, and the cherry on the top of a bad situation.

AFRICA -- freeworldmaps.net:

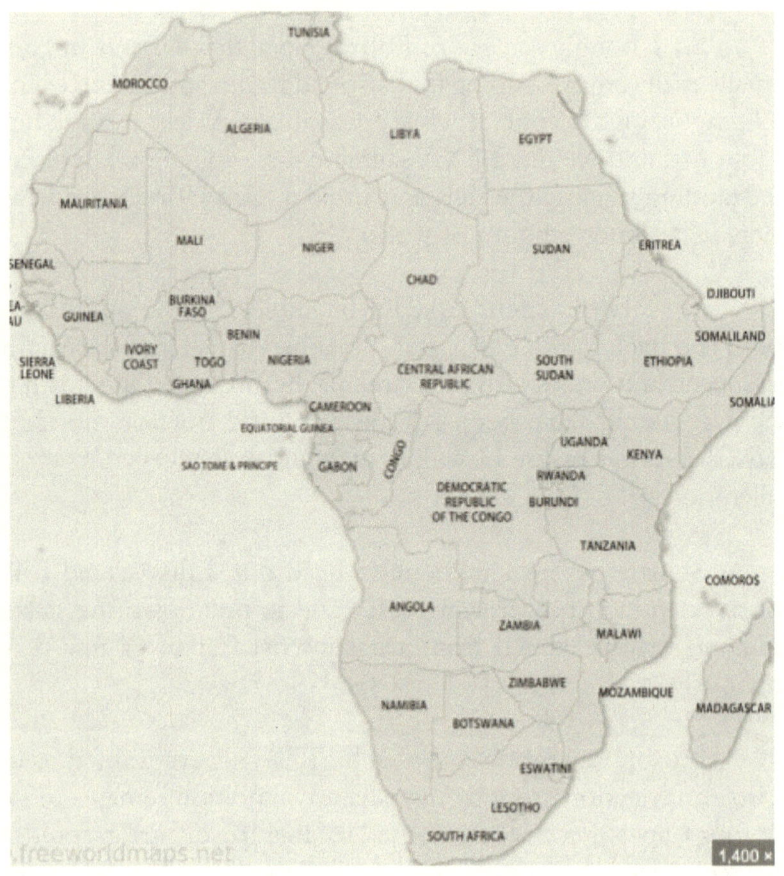

Marvelous fatherland of two good men who have not been allowed to visit it for five years. Y'mean Africa won't let them in? Nah, Australia won't issue them an exit visa. --

13. Saluting a Law Scholar: Wilfred Massingham Seymour

Dr William Russell Massingham Pridgeon (right) being driven to the Brisbane Watchhouse. The Photo: (AAP: Darren England), is from ABC News under the heading "Doctor accused of masterminding child-stealing syndicate…" The other man in the photo is Senior Sgt Darren Williamson.

In the legal profession, we always enjoy saluting a past — or occasionally a present — master of the art. On entering the main building of Harvard Law School, for example, you are greeted by a huge painted portrait of Justice Oliver Wendell Holmes, Jr (1841-1935).

I have only recently discovered the work of Wilfred Massingham Seymour whose main law textbook preceded World War I. Not that I came by it randomly — it was called to my attention by the grandson of the master. The book is entitled: *"Native law and custom; being a compendium of the recognised native customs in force in the native territories of the colony of the Cape of Good Hope."*

It is about the native law of the people of South Africa, and has sparked my interest to find a similar work on the native law of indigenous people in North America, Australia, Philippines, or anywhere. With regard to the Philippines, I'd be curious to find what principles of law were on the books before the unruly takeover by American military forces in 1898, when the territory changed hands as a result of the Spanish-American war.

I confess my racism insofar as I did not know that the customs of South African tribes were as fussy as those of "white man." As set out in Seymour's book, there were provisions, such as breach of contract, if a woman did not go through with a promised marriage. Similarly with the Mabo case in Australia, I have only ever thought of it in terms of white-court activity, featuring our laws of terra nullius. How could I have been so stupid.

Now back to Wilfred Seymour's grandson, namely, Russell Pridgeon. I am unabashedly asking the Aussie legal eagles to tread lightly on this man, Russell, who is currently accused of "conspiracy to defeat the course of justice." Russell hails from a good family. I read in an African Internet article that when Russell's older bro, Geoffrey Pidgeon, also a doctor, met an untimely death in 2017, "people of all races and religions came from far and wide to pay respects" at his memorial in Zimbabwe.

In a criminal trial, the convicted person (and I'm not saying Pridgeon will be convicted) gets a chance to speak up at his sentencing. He can bring character witnesses. (I am thinking of Jahar Tsarnaev's trial where his schoolteachers said Jahar was — to use an Australian word — lovely.) Are you allowed to say "His late grandfather was a bonzer guy"? I don't really know. But here are a couple of paragraphs from Russell Pridgeon's 2023 book, "Everybody Knows: Orchestrating the Theft of Innocence":

"During the Boer War, my maternal grandfather, Wilfred Massingham Seymour, worked for the law firm of "Coghlan and Welsh", as a law clerk, to provide compensation for Boer prisoners of war, sequestered in the British concentration camps in the Cape. He entered the camps and later wrote of what he saw.

"My Grandfather codified traditional native law, so that it became integrated with the Roman Dutch Law used in South African courts. Every Law Student in South Africa from the 1930's to the present time has studied from my Grandfather's text book, Seymour's "Native Law in South Africa", much edited now of course. I learned to have a profound respect for the law from my grandfather and my uncles."

And now to the Preface from Grandpa Seymour's 1911 book. (This comes to us by the miracle of Archive.org, where all sorts of treasures lie waiting for your touch of a button.):

NATIVE LAW AND CUSTOM ... Cape Town 1911

[Dedicated] TO
SENATOR, COLONEL, THE HONOURABLE
WALTER ERNEST MORTIMER STANFORD, C.B., C.M.G.

AS A TRIBUTE TO HIS LONG AND EMINENT SERVICES TO THE INHABITANTS OF THE NATIVE TERRITORIES OF CAPE COLONY, WHILE SECRETARY TO THE NATIVE AFFAIRS DEPARTMENT,

AND AS A TESTIMONY TO THE IMPARTIALITY, JUDICIAL DIGNITY AND INSIGHT INTO NATIVE CUSTOMS WHICH HE DISPLAYED WHILE CHIEF MAGISTRATE OF GRIQUALAND EAST, THIS BOOK is (BY PERMISSION) RESPECTFULLY DEDICATED
BY THE AUTHOR.

PREFACE. [Note: 'kraal' means village.]
The object of this work is to lay before those interested therein the recognised Native customs at present obtaining in the Native Territories of Cape Colony. Legislative enactments and Colonial law are referred to, but only in so far as they affect Native customs.
There is an idea prevailing that the natives in these Terri- tories are not subject to Colonial law, and that cases between them are always decided by the Courts there according to Native customs; but this is not the case. ... It is only in those cases where the obligations between the parties arise out of customs foreign to, and which cannot be dealt with under, Colonial law, that recourse is had to Native law.

Customs have only to a certain extent been recognised by the Courts, as it has been found that some of them are tainted with

slavery, or are adverse to the interests of morality, whilst others are in direct conflict with Proclamations.
For instance, the natives consider that a woman's services to her husband's kraal after his death are one of the considerations for which her dowry is paid, and, according to true or "raw" custom, return of her dowry could be demanded by her deceased husband's people should she leave their kraal; but the courts have refused to allow dowry to be reclaimed on that ground, holding this custom to be detrimental to the welfare of widows.

Knowledge of pure Native law is therefore not of such great importance to the practical lawyer as hitherto. Likewise, the earlier decisions of the courts are of little practical use, and are now often overruled, for they were given at a time when pure Native customs were more or less strictly adhered to, and when the tactful authorities probably deemed it advisable not rigidly to introduce European ideas and improvements into Native customs.

This book is based on decisions of the Supreme Court, and of the Eastern Districts Court (mostly at the time when these Courts had appellate jurisdiction over the Territories), and of the Native Appeal Courts of the Transkei, Tembuland, and East Griqualand (from 1895 to 1909). Statutes, Proclamations, and MacLean's "Compendium of Kaffir Laws and Customs" are also referred to.

The decisions of the Native Appeal Courts referred to in this book will, with some exceptions, be found reported in Henkel's "Native Appeal Courts Reports," or Warner's "Native Appeals," or at the end of this book. It will be seen, from a study of this work, that, speaking generally, the same customs are common to all native tribes. Nevertheless, the name of the tribe, or tribes, to which litigants belonged has been given in all instances where this was indicated in the report of the case. Where a custom is peculiar to one or more tribes the tribal name has been given.

The Author desires to offer his thanks to Mr. A. H. Payn, attorney, of Cape Town, for his advice and help in the revision and arrangement of this work, and to Mr. R. B. Stevenson for reading through, and correcting, the manuscript. M. SEYMOUR. 1910

End of Part 3: Africa// Quotes from Steve Biko (1946- 1977)

The revolutionary sees his task as liberation not only of the oppressed but also of the oppressor. Happiness can never truly exist in a state of tension.

The basic tenet of black consciousness is that the black man must reject all value systems that seek to make him a foreigner in the country of his birth and reduce his basic human dignity.

The great powers of the world may have done wonders in giving the world an industrial look, but the great gift still has to come from Africa - giving the world a more human face.

Apartheid -- both petty and grand -- is obviously evil. Nothing can justify the arrogant assumption that a clique of foreigners has the right to decide on the lives of a majority.

In a bid for change, we have to take off our coats, be prepared to lose our comfort and security, our jobs and positions of prestige and our families. A struggle without casualties is no struggle.

The black man has become a shell, a shadow of man, completely defeated, drowning in his own misery, a slave, an ox bearing the yoke of oppression with sheepish timidity.

Tradition has it that whenever a group of people has tasted the lovely fruits of wealth, security, and prestige, it begins to find it more comfortable to believe in the obvious lie and accept that it alone is entitled to privilege.

A Black man should be more independent and depend on himself for his freedom and not to take it for granted that someone would lead him to it. The blacks are tired of standing at the touchlines to witness a game that they should be playing. They want to do things for themselves and all by themselves.

The most potent weapon of the oppressor is the mind of the oppressed.

(L) Michael Alexander, attorney, Photo: YouTube (C) Dr Mark Trozzi, Photo: torontocaribbean.com (R) Dr Crystal Luchkiw, Photo: barrietoday.com

For comparison to Pridgeon, let's look at another country's way of cancelling a medical license. Dr Trozzi is a physician in Canada who opposes what he sees as the Covid swindle. He does not use that word, but it's a quick way to say that he is a dissident. He runs a website, drtrozzi.org, that delivers good information.

Recently, he reported on a young female doctor who has lost her medical license for having **issued medical exemptions** from the Covid vaccine. It is an uncomplicated case, and it shows the procedure for disbarring a doctor, at least in the province of Ontario.

Worldwide, members of the public were allowed to link into a zoom hearing of the Dr Luchkiw case today, 19 May 2023. Some restrictions were posted, such as "The taking of screenshots is an offense that carries a heavy fine." You can be sure I kept my dear hand off the screenshot button. However, I did see Michael Alexander, attorney for Dr Luchkiw, defending her. He made the statement that her dismissal meant that 1700 patients, some bound for hospice, lost their doctor suddenly, to their disadvantage. An attorney for the College countered by saying that such statements were not in evidence, they were mere assertions and that the members of the Tribunal should consider only the evidence. At the end of the hearing, which lasted about 2.5 hours, the members of the College voted to reserve their decision.

Let's all think critically about the role played by the College. Did Parliament really mean to let a small, unaccountable band of persons decide what the standards of medical practice should be? The

Regulated Health Professions Act, 1991, Schedule 2, provides a Health Professions Procedural Code that establishes a Discipline Committee known as "Ontario Physicians and Surgeons Discipline Tribunal."

On the Tribunal's website: **Mission**: "To hear and decide allegations of physician misconduct and incompetence with independence and fairness, making just decisions in the public interest." Recall that Russell Pridgeon learned, to his chagrin, that if the NSW Medical Council stripped him of his medical license *unlawfully*, they'd face no repercussions. I cannot claim that the Ontario tribunal is sinister. But I *am* saying, let's query any governmental role regarding doctors.

Duty of College. [This is from the Procedural Code] 2.1 It is the duty of the College to work in consultation with the Minister to ensure, as a matter of public interest, that the people of Ontario have access to adequate numbers of qualified, skilled and competent regulated health professionals. [Seems OK]

3 "(1) The College has the following objects: To regulate the practice of the profession and to govern members in accordance with the health profession Act, this Code and the *Regulated Health Professions Act, 1991* and the regulations and by-laws." [Kind of a lot!] *To establish and maintain standards of qualification for persons to be issued certificates of registration." [Re who gets to be a doctor.]

*To develop, establish and maintain standards of professional ethics for the members. [How about an ethic against genocide?] *Any other objects relating to human health care that the Council considers desirable. [Way, way too broad, that. Should be expunged.]

Meetings 7. (1) The meetings of the Council shall be open to the public and reasonable notice shall be given to the members of the College, to the Minister, and to the public. [Goody.] **Exclusion of public** (2) Despite subsection (1), the Council may exclude the public from any meeting or part of a meeting **if it is satisfied** that matters involving public security may be disclosed. [Maybe it could make a court order to prevent such discolures?]

Article at Barrietoday.com, Canadian Newspaper A 20 January 2023 article by Marg Bruineman, in Ontario, reports the first attempt by Luchkiw, and others, to prevent disciplinary action against them. Remember we are talking about Canada here, the land of police breaking the windows of the convoy trucks in the snow, and the land of actual statutes forbidding free speech:

"Dr. Crystal Luchkiw, a Barrie family doctor [and] Trozzi, are accused of making misleading, incorrect or inflammatory [my substitution: correct, vital, and ethical] statements, and about vaccinations, treatments and public health measures concerning COVID-19 through online communications about the pandemic.

"Luchkiw is accused of committing professional misconduct by failing to co-operate with the College of Physicians and Surgeons of Ontario investigation into her infection-control practices ... and issuance of vaccine exemptions. In a motion to the tribunal, the doctors [argued] that the COVID-19 direction issued by their college ... impedes the discussion for informed consent of patients...

"Toronto lawyer Michael Alexander argued that the prosecutions for breaching COVID-19 protocol are unlawful and that the regulatory body doesn't have the authority to investigate, describing the investigations as overbroad "fishing expeditions." In its decision released [in January 2021], the tribunal dismissed suggestions of wrongdoing by the college. **'There is in fact no evidence that anything improper took place during the investigations,'** the five-member panel concluded in a written decision."[bolding added]

I see that that, in October 2021, Dr Luchkiw had to resign her privileges at Royal Hospital since she refused to be vaccinated.

In August 2020, I filed *Maxwell v Secretary of Defense*, in federal district court, protesting any forthcoming mandatory vax. My intention was to illuminate the 1905 Jacobson case, which is often said to be the precedent for forcible vaccination. Not true. Mr Jacobson, in 1905, had to pay a fine for not getting vaccinated but he walked away unvaxxed. I wrote: "The ruling in *Jacobson v Massachusetts* is often cited as precedent on vaccination mandates. Now 116 years old, that ruling needs to be overturned. Much has happened in science to cast doubt on both the efficacy of vaccines and the notion that the unvaccinated person can harm the vaccinated." I also said:

> "Jacobson is widely misinterpreted to mean the Fourth Amendment must bend to a public health emergency. The proper ruling is that of *Home Builders v Blaisdell* (1931); that Court said: 'Emergency does not create power. Emergency does not increase granted power.... The Constitution was adopted in a period of grave emergency. Its grants of power ... were not altered by emergency'."

My case was dismissed faster than you can say "*Blaisdell.*" An appeal to the First Circuit did not get anywhere either.

Now back to Russell Pridgeon's case. He begs us: "Please don't tire of my repeating: Everybody knew about the abuse of these children and nobody did anything. **They know they are above the law.** They do not have a Code of Conduct, they do not have the normal statutory and regulatory obligations in law, that would enable them to be held to account in such a case as mine."

Note: I do not agree with Russell that lack of a code of conduct stands in the way of us holding members of quasi-governmental agencies accountable. The criminal code *is* a code of conduct. Professionals are not exempt. Anyone can do crimes.

Update: Dr Crystal Luchkiw's loss of medical license was confirmed by a July 6, 2023 decision of the College of Physicians and Surgeons of Ontario, the CPSO, mainly as she had out-and-out refused to have her office and her patients' charts inspected by the investigators.

You go, Crystal! I hope many forces will join to recognize what the real problem is. We've all got to stop feeling we are properly 'governed' by private committees and boards (especially of their members have amazing conflicts of interest). Let's practice saying "A forced Pfizer shot is mass murder." I think it's just embarrasssment or awkwardness that make us refrain from saying it.

I wrote to attorney Michael Alexander, JD, today (July 11, 2023), to offer these comments on the Tribunal's 6 July 2023 decision:

1. The 5,000-word decision focuses on Dr Luchkiw's lack of co-operation with the investigators. This shouts that they can't handle a discussion of informed consent, much less about Covid.

2. They said her behavior was "disgraceful, dishonorable or unprofessional." Note the "or." That phrase should not combine all three pejorative terms. One can be *unprofessional* (which also needs defining) and yet not be *disgraceful*, much less *dishonorable.*

3. I am personally conscious of the clever set-ups in government today (US, Australia) that allow non-elected officials to "make law." This is itself **a major issue** and maybe Luchkiw case will bring it to prominence. As I show in my 2013 book, *Consider the Lilies: Review of Cures for Cancer*, the 50 states obeyed AMA regulations about "best practice" that forced doctors to treat cancer by the Big Three (surgery, chemo, and radiation) and by NO OTHER method, no matter how excellently it worked.

4. Thus, the problem there, resulting in millions of unnecessary deaths, really boiled down to the AMA's ability to choke Medicine and Science in this way. So again, with Dr Luchkiw, she is doing something intelligent for a patient, yet a NON-legislative body intervenes to put her out of business. Oh? Isn't the CPS-Ontario a statutory body? Sort of, but it's authorized to make decisions about health (e.g., vaccines) that Parliament never debated.

6. Now to Dr Luchkiw's claim that her patients have a right to informed consent (unequivocal, since Nuremberg Code). If patients do have a right, and if she is asked by CPSO to override it, who is the wrongdoer? I am asking: whose Daddy can beat the other's Daddy up? Can CPSO beat up the people of Ontario?

7. The Tribunal in *Luchkiw* proclaimed : *"... regulated health professionals have no common law, proprietary or constitutional right to practise medicine."* My guess is that they do have a common-law right if the community grants it. Society is the authority. This is too big for CSPO to handle. Note: Criminal behavior by government has no immunity. Many "official" behaviors today are criminal, but our brain can't easily see it.

15. Compare Trials: Jahar Tsarnaev and Russell Pridgeon

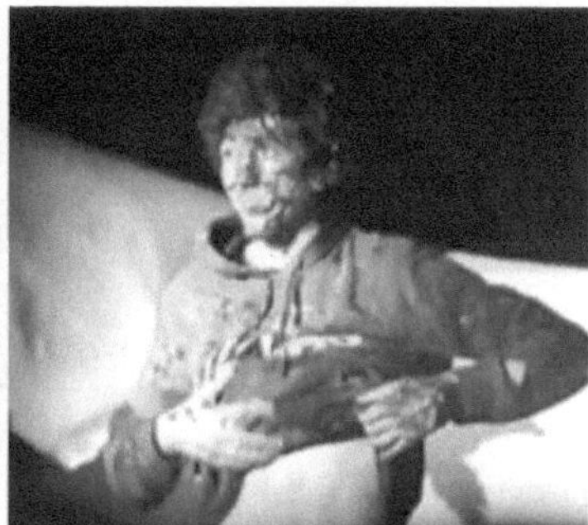

(L) Operation Noetic arrests Patrick O'Dea in 2018, Photo: abc.net.au (Why pixelate the cops?) (R) Jahar Tsarnaev, age 19, at 2013 arrest on a boat, Photo provided by Massachusetts state police

This chapter emphasizes the *deja vu*-ness of the Pridgeon trial to a person (me) who has been very much involved in the Boston Marathon bombing trial, *United States v Tsarnaev.*

Eight Unfair Parts of Dzhokhar ("Jahar") Tsarnaev's Trial
*1. There was no good cause to arrest Jahar. And once he was arrested, the Grand Jury should have realized there was no evidence that he bombed the Marathon. So there should not have been an indictment, much less a trial. The media, however, particularly CNN and the Boston Globe, "filled in" any missing parts, so to speak. The trial began with jury selection and ended with a guilty verdict. The boy has now been on Death Row for 10 years. I blame all Bostonians, including myself, for that ridiculous state of affairs.

*2. Jahar's family wanted him to have an independent lawyer but the Public Defender's office (which is an arm of the Court) prevented that from happening. The Public Defender was Judy Clark. She started her opening statement with the words "It was him." This manner of 'defense' was explained by her supposed wish to get the jury's sympathy for a less-than-death sentence, as "everyone in Boston already knew" he did it thanks to the MSM. (Gee thanks, media.)

*3. The claim that Jahar and his brother Tamerlan carjacked a man, Dun Meng, was evidenced only by Meng's testimony. The brothers had a car and did not need one. During the alleged ride, Meng says Tamerlan boasted that he had just killed a cop at MIT. No one would boast that to a stranger, but it gave media the ability to report that Tamerlan had admitted to that crime. (See what I mean? Like Barbara Olsen and her alleged phone call that established "boxcutters" as the mode of hijacking on 9/11).

*4. Tamerlan Tsarnaev, age 26, did not make it to the trial as he was killed by FBI on April 19, 2013. So how sharply did Defender Clark cross-examine Dun Meng? She didn't. After all, "It was him," so who needs to mount a defense.

*5. Prosecutor gave the following proof of Jahar having bombed the Marathon. First, the FBI offers the "actual" backpack, torn and messy, in which the bomb was allegedly detonated. Its color is black as the ace of spades. Then the FBI offers proof of who did it by showing Jahar walking down the street that day wearing a grayish-white backpack. See? Do you see the connection? No. I don't either.

*6. Two other amici curiae and myself filed a brief which was accepted by the court in 2017, to be used at appeal, regarding the color discrepancy of the two backpacks. Eight lawyers jointly filed another amicus brief to say that Boston was an inappropriate venue for the trial. Their brief, but not ours, was discussed at appeal. Silence is golden, i'in it?

*7. There's plenty more. Read my book "Boston's Marathon Bombing: What Can Law Do?" -- I want to get quickly to the Pridgeon affair.

*8. Oh wait, one more thing about your basic non-bomber Muslim patsy. When I was giving a lecture at Watertown Library in 2018 (a moot court in which I played the Defender), a lawyer in the audience told me that there was a 2018, *McCoy v Louisiana*, in which the US Supreme Court ruled that a defense attorney cannot override the direction of the accused by deciding to admit guilt for him. Of course I ran to tell this to the Boston federal appeals court but the silence was just as golden as ever.

The Long Road to a Pridgeon Trial

Unlike the Tsarnaev brothers who did nothing in connection with a Marathon, Russell Pridgeon actually did do what the police say he did. In fact he announced that he did it. He wrote the details, in English (and with good grammar, too), and sent it to such persons as the Minister for Child Safety Di Farmer, and the CDPP, i.e., the Commonwealth Director of Public Prosecutions.

Pridgeon wrote: "Two girls are in hiding because of terrible abuse by the father. Will you please help?" The said Minister **blocked his emails**. I think we can agree that such silence is golden. Or maybe platinum.

One difference between the trials of Jahar and Russell is that Jahar's occurred smack on two years after the bombing, while Russell's got delayed and delayed. It's been four and a half years so far and who knows if the government will ask for a further extension. [Oops, they just did, till October 2023.] During three of the four years he had the pleasure (well, it would be quite a pleasure if he were into S&M) of wearing a leg bracelet to track his every move.

There was no good legal reason for the leg affair. But don't forget media coverage. Oh, I didn't describe it: On October 2018, the police, or the media, made Russell out to be a kingpin of an abduction syndicate. And one who dealt in the "proceeds of crime" and had sent a million dollars to God knows where and had numerous passports, and maybe a false nose like Jimmy Durante so he could escape on a yacht.

OK, I lied about the false nose, but the aura of flight riskiness was enough to make the leg tracker appear to be based on sensible law instead of S&M.

Wait, wait. There's a comparative to Jahar, whose elderly aunt, Rosa Tsarnaeva, came over from Russia to give him a character reference. She was closely guarded by Boston police, at a budget motel, all the while wearing one of those things. Why didn't Bostonians object? After all, we Boston Irish Catholics know right from wrong. (I got a heavy dose of it starting at the Baptismal font, does it show?)

Well, who is going to feel for the aunt of a terrorist? Aunty could be a terrorist herself for all we knew. Don't let her disappear into the population, as she might have a couple of bombs in *her* backpack. Plus, "Jihadists are all alike." Etc.

Dr Russell Pridgeon has gone nuts over the fact that the police have signed affidavits saying that a certain little boy did NOT report abuse when in fact he did, including reports ***to*** the police. You can take that to be an element of unfairness to Russell, but Russell sees it as unfairness to the boy. He harps on it.

By the way, Dee McLachlan, comforter of dozens of mothers, could give you a stack of examples where the mandatory reporters did their duty, but their reports get "lost". That's actually a crime and we don't need to go back in time to Sir William Blackstone to find it. In the American idiom, it's codified as a federal statute at 18 USC 1519. (To look up any US law, google for the offense, plus "18 USC." The codifying states the issue precisely):

> "Whoever knowingly alters, destroys, mutilates, conceals, covers up, falsifies, or makes a false entry in any record, document, or tangible object with the intent to impede, obstruct, or influence the investigation or proper administration of any matter within the jurisdiction of any department or agency of the United States … or in contemplation of any such matter or case, shall be fined under this title, imprisoned not more than 20 years, or both."

Here is another example of tampering with evidence, and it's quite clever. The technique does not have a name yet, as it has only been technologically feasible for a while. Let's say you tape your camera under your car. Drive a few miles. It will record the tarmac, right? Then print all the frames, each with a date and time stamp. Voila! Heaps of evidence with which to load up the file against the man accused of having given the children a ride from A to B.

Russell is sure that this was done to make the "Brief of Evidence" hard for him to read through. In his book *Everybody Knows*, Dr Pridgeon moans (with emphasis added by me):

"On 31 May 2019 I asked the presiding magistrate to order the CDPP to provide the particularization for each defendant for each charge. The Magistrate ordered the CDPP to do this by 31 July 2019. This did not happen. The **CDPP completely failed to obey court orders**."

[Note: In Australia, the police and the prosecuting barrister are the same team, or the very same person. Here is Rule 82 from the Qld Barristers Rules: "A prosecutor must fairly assist the court to arrive at the truth, **must seek impartially to have the whole of the relevant evidence placed intelligibly before the court**…."]

Russell writes in his soon-to-be famous book: "The CDPP do not expect to be taken to task or held to account. They became angry when I dared to tell the Court what their behaviour was, and what it should be. **Astonishingly, they have no expectation that they would be reported to the Legal Services Board**, where, because of the dishonesty component of their behaviour, **they should be struck off**."

Moreover, there are **mirroring laws in Qld's Criminal Code** 1899, to mirror the Barristers rules. See Section 590AB "Disclosure obligation," which reinforce these obligations and give them force of law. Dr Pridgeon says: **"Every law student should be digging into these now to see what charges they can envision."**

A Beautiful Statement by Police. I wish to let you know how AFP Commander Crime Paul Osborne feels about the crimes of Pridgeon, O'Dea and the others. Osborne wrote:

> "Laws such as these are designed to safeguard the integrity of our judicial system and to protect those vulnerable people who are involved in proceedings before the Courts, including the Family Court of Australia. The AFP **will not hesitate to act on criminal offences that ultimately deprive children of the opportunity to lead a normal life**, regardless of their particular family situation." Excellent! Spot on! You win, Commander.

Postscript: Talk about graphical impact! When I looked at the two photos, at top of this chapter, of Patrick and Jahar, the thought came to me "Two men making an arrest" -- I mean it could be a photo of Patrick O'Dea and Jahar each doing a ***citizen's*** arrest. Patrick was catching the real child-stealers.

Jahar could easily have arrested the dozens of cops who were shooting at him. (And the one who subsequently knifed his neck.) They were breaking the law. Gotcha!

In Massachusetts, to justify making a citizen's arrest, it's required that you see a felony happening, or know that it has happened, and that your quarry is the felon. The felony -- back then on 19 April 2019 in Watertown -- was the assault being committed by those who are shooting an unarmed nineteen-year-old.

Technically, the arrestor (Jahar) should say "I am citizen's-arresting you for assault and grievous bodily harm." There is no requirement to read your quarry his/her Miranda's. Ah, that's good, as it probably wasn't feasible for Jahar, when lying on the ground with a knife in his neck, and his jaw smashed by gunshot, to say "Officer(s), you don't have to say anything but whatever you do say may be used in court against you. K?"

But even if it only sounded like "Gurgle, gurgle," that might suffice. The relevant maxim is "Apices juris non sunt jura": The niceties of the law are not the law."

16. Did a Prince Order the Elimination of a Whistleblower?

(L) Former Canadian G-G, David Johnston, (C) King Charles' equerry Major Johnny Thompson, (R) Kevin Annett, Eagle Strong Voice

I have just received an email from Republic of Kanata, related to the innovative work of Kevin Annett of Canada. Annett has, for 24 years, been running tribunals -- peoples' tribunals -- against officials of church and state. He is also a leader in the fight against satanic rituals, in which children are sometimes killed.

Today, 29 May 2023, Annett announced that an "insider" has come forward with testimony that the then Prince of Wales, in late December 2010, ordered the murder of a whistleblower named William Combes in Canada. Combes had stated that back in 1964 he saw Queen Elizabeth and Prince Philip choose, and take away, 10 kids (7 boys, 3 girls), from a residential school for indigenous kids in Kamloops, British Columbia.

The ***dramatis personae*** in the Insider's affidavit are as follows:

*King Charles (at the time, Prince Charles),
*William Combes, the whistleblower, of the Queen's visit, whose life ended on 26 **February 2011** (12 years ago) in St Paul's Hospital, Vancouver,
*Nurse Chloe Kirker, who saw Combes die and said it was by arsenic poisoning,
*Major Johnny Thompson, platoon commander, currently the King's equerry (was age 28 at time of the 2011 incident),
*David Johnston, Governor General of Canada, 2011 to 2017,
*William JS Elliot, Commissioner of the RCMP (Mounties) from 2007 to November 2011,

*and The Insider, who signed the affidavit on May 16, 2023 (his name is not yet provided to us), a British army officer and member of the monarch's security team.

Here is the announcement, verbatim, in Annett's words:

London: The present King of England, Charles Windsor, ordered the killing of the only living eyewitness to his mother Queen Elizabeth's abduction of ten aboriginal children, according to a former officer of the British Army and the monarchy's security team.

In a legal affidavit dated May 16, 2023, and issued to the ICLCJ, this officer states that in late December of 2010, he participated in a "special operations" meeting in Buckinghamshire to plan the murder of William Combes. The meeting was called by Major Jonny [sic] Thompson of the Royal Regiment, who was the security advisor to the then-Prince of Wales, Charles Windsor.

According to the affidavit [by the Insider]

"Major Thompson told us he was appearing on behalf of his Majesty the Prince of Wales [in December 2011] who had ordered the elimination of a foreign assassin threatening the royal family. I was surprised at the time [2011] that such an order was not being handled through MI6 and its overseas contractors. I was even more surprised when the target was a Canadian Red Indian, since normally the RCMP have jurisdiction over such operations.

"When one of my colleagues raised this point with Major Thompson, he replied, *"The Mounties will handle this one on the ground. We're just setting the wheels in motion. This is a royal directive with the knowledge and consent of the Canadian Governor General, Mr. Johnston."* It was later confirmed to me that in early February 2011, Canada's RCMP Commissioner, a Mr. Elliott, dispatched a squad of operatives to Vancouver to deal with the target.

"I also learned later that the Indian they had killed was a Mr. William Combes, who as a homeless man seemed an unlikely terrorist. But when I read of Combes' statement regarding his witnessing of the Queen's apparent abduction of ten Indian children in Kamloops in 1964 and of how he was to speak about that incident before a public tribunal in London in the spring of 2011, I could understand although not condone the action of Prince Charles in taking Mr. Combes off the board."

On February 24, 2011, William Combes was forcibly detained by RCMP officers in Vancouver and incarcerated against his will in St. Paul's Catholic hospital. He died there two days later of arsenic poisoning, according to his attending nurse Chloe Kirker. See her: https://www.youtube.com/watch?v=Dd5-oH9RELM&t=678s

My Opinion

Kevin Annett is one of very few people who, upon realizing that governments are rigged, has established a new Republic, the Republic of Kanata. (That's the native name for a place that later gave its name to the country, Canada.)

Annett was a United Church priest in the 1990s who was informed, by his indigenous parishioners, that their kids had been forced into "residential schools" throughout the 20th century, and many died. (Kids don't normally die, do they?) Kevin then went through all the correct means of reporting this (see his book *Unrepentant*) but got only personal attacks for doing so.

A few years ago, he came out with a story about a man, William Combes, who had been a resident in one of the schools in 1964 to which indigenous kids were forcibly taken. Combes claimed that he actually saw the Queen of England come to the school to shop for kids. I was pretty skeptical, and said so, as a visit from the Queen to her realms is usually filled with media attention.

There was only this one witness still alive, Combes, and he was *allegedly* killed in a hospital on February 2011, after proclaiming his story. Thus, I thought we'd have to leave it as a permanent "maybe." But now, apparently on his own initiative, an Insider in the British Army reports that the "elimination" of Combes was "a royal order."

I have been more or less consumed since 2005 with a search for ways to get around the problem of our having a secret government in the US. Believe me, I can show you umpteen examples of the law enforcement personnel in top levels of the Department of Justice, seeming to live a surreal existence.

Or should I say, the naive public lives a surreal life, accepting the ever-false words of the powerful -- or choosing to submit rather than question. So this story provides an amazing breakthrough. I can't think of another with such potential impact.

Kids. At the same time, because I got into researching the CIA's mind control program, MK-Ultra, I became aware of the uses to which children were horribly put. It's not all directed by government -- "satanic ritual sacrifice" goes back many centuries.

At this very moment in Australia the police are prosecuting (yes, in Australia the police can prosecute) a doctor named Russell Pridgeon, whom I can unequivocally vouch for as a good guy. Really, the prosecutor must have a low IQ that he would make such a blunder as to accuse Pridgeon of crimes connected to "child trafficking," when it is the police and courts that do it.

So, in general, the schemes that Annett has been reporting -- genocide in the indigenous schools, and also satanic rituals in many countries -- must not be ignored. His solution is to form a sort of shadow government, in which he applies common law. The name of his group is International Tribunal for Crimes of Church and State. The website is www.itccs.org. It seems to have been scrubbed. Natch. Annett's books are in libraries, luckily.

What Action Can Be Taken?

Before you tell me to stop dreaming of the Tooth Fairy, I want to make a simple list of what legal measures are theoretically available -- on the proviso that the Insider really did swear an affidavit. The first step is for some government -- I guess it may have to be Annett's Republic of Kanata -- to arrange an investigation. Witnesses would be commanded to come forward. Let's *pretend* that all the players listed above do answer the call.

We are looking for guilt. Two persons who are said to have had a role to play in the death of William Combes are: the Governor General and the Mounty Police Commissioner -- respectively, David Johnston and William JS Eliott. It will be valuable to get their agreement that they did know about a planned operation.

Each of them could say, plausibly, that they were told to get rid of a man who was *a threat to the life* of the monarch. Combes would thus be painted as a criminal. I guess they could plead that they had no backgrounder on the fellow's having witnessed the queen (with Prince Philip) "shopping for children."

Don't forget, our Insider heard the story in Buckinghamshire. From there, the kill Order went out; the two Canadians do NOT have to have been made aware of how or why a decision was made to terminate the life of William Combes.

Note: We do have one other Insider who can be subpoena'd to testify: our Insider says his "Colleague" raised the question of why MI6 wasn't being used. Let's ask that colleague to assure us that he really did ask such a question. Now what of Major Johnson? He is Charles' equerry now, but according to Annett was security adviser to the then to the then-Prince of Wales.

Now we're talkin' accomplice. Major is high enough rank to have been briefed on all aspects of the Kamloops incident. A "security advisor to the heir apparent" isn't a dumb-dumb. But he could plausibly say "We had to kill the man because he was spreading a *false* story about Her Majesty" rather than "We had to shut him up so the whole child-stealing caper isn't blown sky high."

Now we come to the king. Under law, the king can do no wrong. If you see him carjack a bus, just look the other way, please. This 100% immunity will make the lawyers say "Hands off." However, Charles was not king when he ordered the death of Combes, he was only "HRH." So he is (arguably) not immune.

Although the affidavit says the operation was ordered by the Prince of Wales, I suspect it was ordered by a power *higher* than

Charles, such as the members of the Order of the Garter. Or Klaus Schwab. Or whoever runs the scheme to steal kids.

I offer a salute to four great whistleblowers: William Combes, Nurse Chloe Kirkner, Rev Kevin Annett, and the Insider. You go, guys! Thanks for helping kids who right this minute are enslaved. Ain't gonna be enslaved much longer! Note: I take Annett to be an honest activist and to have done his homework. Years ago, I corresponded with his Dad on matters unrelated to kidnap. I know Kevin is from a good family.

Postscript. After the above was published, someone congratulated me on proving that the queen did such-and-such at Kamloops. I most certainly did not prove it. No one has proved it. All that can be said is that allegedly we now have a sworn accusation that Prince Charles in 2010 ordered the death of Combes.

I am slow to accept a conspiracy theory, in order to protect my reputation regarding events that I claim to be false flags, and which I have researched sufficiently to draw a conclusion. I fully claim that the 2013 Marathon bombing, the 2014 Sydney siege, and the 1996 Port Arthur massacre were false flags. I know for sure that cancer cures were suppressed from 1890 onwards. I'm 99% sure that no one died at Sandy Hook in 2012. And please write me down as a full-on believer that the 2020 pandemic was malicious. Here are relevant books authored by Yours Truly:

Consider the Lilies: 18 Cures for Cancer and Their Legal Status (2013)
Port Arthur: Enough is Enough (co-authored by Dee McLachlan (2015)
Inquest: Siege in Sydney (2017)
Boston's Marathon Bombing: What Can Law Do? (2021)
Unreality: Sandy Hook Messes Minds (2022)
Elias Davidsson: Palestinian Jew and 9/11 Truther (2023)

Update: An admired whistleblower, Dr Rashid Buttar, has been killed. How do we know it was not a natural death? Because he told us of threats against him and he monitored his poisoning. He helped autistic kids and so did Dr Jeff Bradstreet whose death was outrageously called suicide. Don't let this go unpunished!

17. Rachel Hits Brick Wall of Police Arrogance

(L) Rachel blew the whistle at age 9 (C) Rachel testifies to ITNJ and Shaun Attwood's video (R) Louise Bell, age 8, died 1983, Photo: AAP

Rachel Vaughan was born into the MacIntyre family in Adelaide in 1973. Her father, known as Max, was probably the murderer of Rachel's half-sister Clare, a potential tattler who was found in the backyard with a broken neck, yet said to have suicided. That has never held Rachel back from doing her duty to society. An older brother, Andrew, has also worked hard at revealing truths.

I believe Rachel has succeeded where other have failed. Granted she has not yet brought about changes in the police, but she always names names and confronts the wrongdoers. She has also withstood a remarkable onslaught of criticism. At least one troll follows her industriously on the Internet.

Yesterday I asked Google for "Rachel Vaughan, Australia." The first page was filled with American Rachel Vaughans. Yet the very top entry was a Facebook page that is devoted to insulting and "fact-checking" discouraging our Rachel. Doesn't it cost a lot to get top billing on Google? Who is paying for it? Why?

As if we didn't know. Two famous murders that involve Max (who died at age 89 in 2017) are Adelaide lore. One is the disappearance of the three Beaumont children in 1966. The other is the death of Louise Bell, a playmate of Rachel's, whose death by knife, at the hands of Max, was personally witnessed by Rachel. A different man, Dieter Pfennig, is in prison for that crime, based on the usual flimsy but media-heavy evidence. Does anyone in South Australia give a damn about wrongful convictions?

From Rachel's notebook -- a tiny sample of her contacts:

April ***2006:*** *STATUTORY DECLARATION:* Max's assault on me with knife, saw a mutilated child in Macklin St bathroom.

June ***2007:*** Letter to many MPs re lack of investigation by the SA Police, naming Max as the body boy for 'the Family,' also to **Doug Barr, Major Crime** and Det. Supt. Phillip Hoff.

8 Aug ***2007:*** *RESPONSE*: letter from **Paul Holloway**, Minister for Police. "No evidence linking Allan McIntyre" to this.

21 Aug ***2007:*** *INTERVIEW* with Annette Burden and Scott Barker, SCIB, detailing abuse of me and witness child's dismembered body as well as a man's right foot, 1977.

5 Sept ***2007:*** Told MPs: Jane Lomax-Smith, Michael Atkinson, Jay Weatherill, Carmel Zollo, Nick Xenophon, Kris Hannah.

20 Sept ***2007:*** *RESPONSE* from Police Complaint Authority: **"*cannot justify commitment of personnel and resources.*"** [See?]

8 Feb ***2008:*** 4th letter sent to officials re SAPOL refusal to act on our allegations.

Sept ***2009:*** Statutory Declaration that I saw a young girl being killed under my house in 1983, and Max filmed us together.

23 Feb ***2012***: My **letter to SCIB asks why my late sister Clare's psychiatrist wasn't questioned re her allegations**

19 Jan ***2012:*** Told Crimestoppers' Louise Bell is buried at 8 Macklin St., Edwardstown, under a slab of concrete.

Rachel: In SA, there were a few good cops who did their best to help me along the way. I am grateful for their help.

Report. ***November 23, 2019*** —"Receive a message from a friend that the little shed/mouse house at Macklin Street is being jackhammered up. I contact Dee McLachlan in Melbourne and friends in Adelaide and tell them what is happening.

"I race into Adelaide and arrive at Macklin St. I can hear the jackhammer going. A skip in the driveway is full of rubble. I try to speak to current owner about the fact that he is digging up a crime scene and it needs to be done forensically: scene of death of Louise Bell. He says he's contacted police and whistles.

"Female owner comes out. She knows my name, asks me what I'm doing there. I explain that I am there as I have been waiting 36 years for this day and I am hoping for some closure. My supporter speaks for me, asks that I be allowed to go out the back and watch the dig or take some soil – for closure. 'No.'

"We go to my car and get in to leave. Police turn up as we attempt to leave and flash their lights blocking my egress. They say that I cannot return to Macklin Street for 24 hours. Friends and I go to Railway Terrace and knock to see if the owner is home. 'Easements' indicated on 1955 property titles which look like tunnels. Nothing ensued. We're still eager for action elsewhere."

There is no reason in the world why the citizenry of Adelaide cannot demand and get an exhumation of certain bodies at Stansbury. There is no reason in the world why all the negligent cops can't be held accountable. There is no reason not to teach ethics at the police academy. The Ethics lecture would go like this:

> Dear Rookies, You may have heard, in your very first week, that there are some heavies in the force whom you should not mess with. That is a bad directive. We need to clean this place up. Why suffer intimidation? Let us do the intimidating, with your help.
>
> We have guns, tasers, tear gas, handcuffs, a lockup, some date rape drugs. Nabbing roughies is our bread and butter. If you don't think you've got the guts, please work elsewhere. Just remember, the bad guys think they have rights. Surprise -- they don't!

18. Witness-Tampering Killed Troy Davis

(L) Martina Correia with nuns in Dublin (C) the back of the famous tee-shirt (R) Troy Davis (1968-2011)

Let us look at the problem of witness tampering. I suspect that some witnesses in the Pridgeon/O'Dea case have been "influenced." Let's walk through the Troy Davis case, which demonstrates *judicial malfeasance* as the means of getting Troy executed.

We all knew Troy was innocent. Here are two ways you could know it. First, a worldwide group of justice warriors took up his case and gathered two-thirds of a million signatures, requesting clemency. Among the requesters were Bishop Tutu, former president Jimmy Carter, and 3,000 clergypersons. Clemency only means reduce his sentence form death to life imprisonment. There was no reason for 3 of 5 members of Georgia's Pardon Bord to vote against such a strong request. So that's Red Flag #1.

The other Red Flag is the fact that another man was suspected of having been the person who actually committed the crime. Even his cousin blames him. But the police, to this day, have never charged that man or investigated him in any way. It's clear that officials didn't want to solve the crime (a fatal shooting of security guard Mark McPhail). They wanted Troy removed from society.

The police wanted to blame Troy, so they set up 9 people to give false testimony at his trial. Later, but before Troy was executed, seven of the nine recanted their testimony. An eighth was deceased (I think, not sure) and the ninth (I think) was the man I mentioned who likely "did it."

Recantations by Six 'Eyewitnesses' Whose Original 1991 Testimony Had Been Used To Convict Troy Davis

Antoine Williams: They asked me to describe the shooter and what he looked like and what he was wearing. I kept telling them that I didn't know. It was dark, my windows were tinted, and I was scared. .... After the officers talked to me, they gave me a statement and told me to sign it. I signed it. I did not read it because I cannot read.

Kevin McQueen: The truth is that Troy never confessed to me... I made up the confession from information I had heard on TV.

Jeffrey Sapp: I got tired of them harassing me, and they made it clear that the only way they would leave me alone is if I told them what they wanted to hear. I told them that Troy told me he did it, but it wasn't true. ... I didn't want to have any more problems with the cops, so I testified against Troy.

Darrell Collins: After a couple of hours of the detectives yelling at me and threatening me, I finally broke down and told them what they wanted to hear. They would tell me things that they said had happened and I would repeat whatever they said. ... the police had me so messed up that I felt that's all I could do or else I would go to jail.

Dorothy Ferrell: From the way the officer was talking, he gave me the impression that I should say that Troy Davis was the one who shot the officer like the other witness had .... I also felt like I had to cooperate with the officer because of my being on parole.... The truth was that I didn't see who shot [MacPhail].

Larry Young: I couldn't honestly remember what anyone looked like or what different people were wearing. Plus, I had been drinking that day, so I just couldn't tell who did what. The cops didn't want to hear that and kept pressing me to give them answers. They made it clear that we weren't leaving until I told them what they wanted to hear ....

Troy's family was elated when each of the 7 said they had lied, due to police pressure. Recanting was risky. It meant he/she had originally committed perjury and could face punishment now.

So what happened after that? Troy filed a habeas corpus claim with the US Supreme Court. That court in turn asked the local Georgia Judge to take another look at the recantations. I can only assume that this judge, Judge Moore, was under instructions to murder Troy, so to speak. He found all seven statements to be unusable. It is a great embarrassment to read what he said:

-- Moore refers to "live, credible testimony" from police and prosecutor, as though it were of the same type as disinterested testimony. This is unheard of.

-- Moore never says that, in the document he is reviewing, some recanters mention being "threatened with guns." Amazing.

-- He misrepresents the defense's effort to subpoena Sylvester Coles, and **fails to say** that some identify Coles as the killer.

-- Finding no other way to make the police coercion go away he discredits it: "Police would have coerced better than that." [!!!] Please re-read that sentence.

What's the law here? We can easily agree that various police persons tampered with the witnesses originally. Witness tampering consists either of bribing someone to give false testimony or pressuring someone to NOT be a witness, or to tune down, or alter, his testimony. Georgia's legislation provides [bolding added]:

GA Code sec 16-10 (2020) "A person who, with intent to **deter a witness from testifying freely, fully, and truthfully to any matter pending in any cour**t, ... communicates, directly or indirectly, to such witness any **threat** of injury or damage to the person, property, or employment of the witness ... or who offers or delivers any **benefit**, reward, or consideration to such witness or to a relative or associate of the witness shall, upon conviction thereof, be punished by imprisonment for not less than one year"

Troy Davis's feisty sister Martina died 6 weeks after his execution, but the younger sister Kimberly Davis has survived and intends to get justice for her brother. I think Judge Moore is to blame for not reversing the decision about the witnesses, but I also think each of the police needs to be investigated for their alleged witness-tampering. Why ever not? They committed a plain crime.

Mainly, I think it is the US Supreme Court's fault, as I always wish to blame the top person the most. Indeed, I suspect that a decision about Troy was made at a level *higher* than SCOTUS. Recall again the low-level Pardon Board three persons who forbade clemency. One of those three, Gale Buckner, became head of Commission on Juvenile Justice 2 months after Troy died and then became a chief magistrate. Who influenced her, and why?

Now let's talk about Australian law, with an eye to the Operation Noetic fandangle. Per the Commonwealth CRIMES ACT 1914, sec 36A

Intimidation of witnesses etc (1) A person (the ***first person***) commits an offence if: (a) the first person: (i) threatens, intimidates or restrains another person; or (ii) uses violence to, or inflicts an injury on, another person; or

(iii) causes or procures violence, damage, loss or disadvantage to another person; or (iv) **causes or procures the punishment of another person**; and

(b) the first person does so on account of the other person having appeared, or being about to appear, as a witness in a judicial proceeding. Penalty: Imprisonment for 5 years.

I can't confirm any hanky-panky regarding witnesses in the trial of the Noetic case. In fact, I am not sure of anything that is happening in that case, thanks to suppression orders! That trial has something to do with relatives of abused kids "stealing" the kid and thus breaching custody orders. Perhaps government witnesses, such as from Child Protection agencies, are the likely targets of pressure. Why do they claim that a kid is NOT suffering abuse, when it's plain as the nose on your face that he IS? Did they get bribed or coerced to give false witness? Are they sadists?

As I report in my *Reunion* book, Adam Sauer, a young judge in the Iowa district court, refused to accept the testimony of a CPS social worker, Ms Chelsea Gray, age 30, in regard to the (unnecessary) placing of four siblings in foster care. An agent for the Division of Criminal Investigation, Scott Reger, signed the affidavit outlining how Ms Gray had given false testimony under oath. He lists three counts of perjury. Per Newsobserver.com:

-- She testified at a hearing that she had spoken with their teachers about academic and social concerns the kids were exhibiting at school. Later she admitted that she had not spoken to teachers.

-- She testified that she went to the foster home to check on the children once a month, as required by law, but later admitted she did not visit them.

-- She testified that she would recommend a foster care placement keeping all 4 children in the same home, but it was found that she had in mind to separate one of the children from the other three.

Maybe that excellent judge, Adam Sauer, could have gone further to find out *why* Ms Gray lied.

In his book *Everybody Knows*, Dr Russell Pridgeon discusses the false evidence about his passport that was stated by police and false evidence about his finances. But in every chapter of the book, Pridgeon throws a fit over what is NOT being said.

Namely, the officials never exercise their larynx to discuss the children's fate. It is a total nonissue in the Noetic Operation. I now propose that -- although it does not appear in black-letter law -- **the whole unreality of this behavior may have a tamper-like effect on every witness**. People are dissuaded from saying anything contrary to this big unreal 'Noetic' scenario. Do you know what I mean? We all lean greatly to social conformity.

19. We Are in Desperate Times, As Never Before

(L) Photo: geoengineeringwatch.org (R) Sonic weapons, Photo: abc.net.au

Folks are very shy to say it, because it sounds "over the top," but we are in trouble as never before. And should embarrassment about saying that something is over the top really control us?

I'll list here any disasters I can think of -- most of which were already discussed or alluded to in previous chapters.

1. Things connected to the main theme: child trafficking:

Worldwide there is a commercial traffic in, of all things, kids!

The kids live a life of fear and sometimes physical abuse or sexual abuse and will pay the price for it during their whole lives.

If a mother reports sexual abuse by the father, she instantly becomes a target of courts, police, psychologists and CPS's.

Although laws are in place to prevent all this, *judges* won't comply. They gag the audience, they twist the facts, they act meanly.

Elected representatives have been silent, except Georgia Senator Nancy Schaefer who was shot dead with her husband for trying.

The history of mind control via cults and via programming such as in the "experimental" MK-Ultra is vaguely connected to this.

Australian lawyers who complain, such as Maurice Kriss, George Potkonyak, or Serene Teffaha, get penalized by government. The control over the whole situation is fantastic and un-knowable.

2. Globalist Tyranny by WHO and Others

Life has been difficult for many populations, and at times the US is the cause of the suffering. We "regime change" to suit our needs. We grab resources (Jimmy Carter said the US has a 'right' to Middle East oil.) We do bombings without Congress' say-so.

There are also globalist players who run the world, including the US. They control banking. The Bank of England gets to set the price of gold. George Soros can lower the value of any currency.

There is a new plan already partly in effect, to eliminate cash and make everyone's spending habits known to the bankers who will assign a credit score to citizens, threatening them with starvation if they do not obey humiliating rules. We will stop being free.

From 2020 to 2023, a little-understood part of the UN, the World Health Organization, falsely claimed emergency powers for itself such as to order a lockdown of nonessential businesses.

Almost all national leaders, including Trump and Biden, and the UK's Boris Johnson, acted to obey as if there were no issue of the proper role for WHO to play. They all kowtowed! It appears to have been a globalist move by any other name.

Most citizens took the pandemic seriously and wore masks, getting hostile with people who were not "Covid responsible."

Some doctors -- Vernon Coleman in UK, Peter McCullough in US, Thomas Borody in Australia, Sucharit Bhakdi in Germany, and many others recognized the mass murder being committed.

There were intense efforts at censorship by the press, with efforts to criminalize "misinformation." Canadian physician Mark Trozzi lost his medical license. Nurses who spoke out lost their job.

Then there came the effort to get the whole world vaccinated. John Magufuli, president of Tanzania may have lost his life for protesting. Australian Aboriginals were forcibly vaccinated.

Mike Yeadon, former CEO of Pfizer, said it was a deliberate kill.

3. The Takeover of Culture by Bill Gates and Others

Someone had already been trying to weaken society by attacking religion, family, and nationalism throughout the 20th century, but this was disguised as 'goody' efforts, notably within communism.

It had begun by the time of the French Revolution in 1789, and was done, with utter force, by the Bolsheviks in 1917. Unknown to most Americans, the US helped Commies win China in 1949.

It continued in the US itself quietly such as by holding back on proper teaching in school. Today, kids are controlled by devices.

Marriage was discouraged in movies and TV; having children out of wedlock is now the norm. Stepfamilies are almost the norm.

Bill Gates seems to have anointed himself Lord of what we eat. There will be bugs for dinner, preceded by no debate on the subject. He is buying up land to control agriculture, and farmers in the Netherlands have been told to find other occupations! In Australia, the government has killed bees in hives for no reason.

Geo-engineering, 5G Technology, and God Knows What

Since 1945, we have been able to create tsunamis and in the 1960s the US announced its rain-making and plans to control weather, which also entails control of crops. Until recently, all mentions of geoengineering were laughed at, but then admissions were made that governments have filled the skies with some chemicals or bacteria as a way of limiting "climate change." Again, such decision that affect 8 billion people were made by a handful. We don't know their names or their further plans, but had better find out!

There is cause to worry in regard to the massive 5G towers that were installed during the pandemic. Oz law will forbid mention of 5G concerns as 'misinformation.' (That clinches it for me.) Space-denial weapons are used to make people run away to avoid pain. This was done to protesters in Canberra in 2023. For shame! I think techies come up with Artificial Intelligence mainly because it is possible -- which is not a rational reason to do something.

End of Part Four: Kafka// A Song: "Jahar on the MTA," by Mary Maxwell, public domain (JaharCompletelyInnocent.com)

1. America needs to hear 'bout a man named Tsar-NA-ev, and his capture in Watertown. Jahar had no way to know that himself and his bro would be suspects of a Marathon bomb. Will he ever return? Will the prisoner return? His fate is currently sealed. We need lots of good people to stop acting like sheeple, and get the truth revealed!

2. Tamerlan was NOT 'run over,' and was never in a shootout, on that April 19th morn. He was shown on CNN -- the FBI escorted him -- as naked as the day he was born. Will he ever return? Bro can never return. His 26 years are through. He hoped to be a boxing star. His Dad thought he'd go far. And for Todashev, the same is true.

3. Boston Globe declared the bomber was hiding in a boat. He had penciled a confession on deck! Troopers shot 200 bullets, at the un-armed suspect. And Jeff Campbell said, "They knifed his neck." Will he ever return? Will Maret's nephew return? The injustice is still un-learned. It took masterful collusion, to arrive at "execution" -- a sentence that he DID NOT earn.

4. Ja-HAR had some classmates, down at U-Mass Dartmouth, who could give him an alibi. They got rounded up real fast. Some were jailed and harassed. So, they could not testify.

Will he ever return? Will Dzhok-har return? Some say his chances are slim. All it takes is one "OK." It could happen any day. Then his murder will 'LEGALLY' begin. [guitar interlude]

5. Gov'nor Patrick made a robo call, to everybody's cell phone, to announce a bit of martial law. Soldiers beat on doors, as their Humvees roared. You might have thought it was war.

Will he ever return? Yes, if witnesses come forward. If you know who killed Collier, please 'sing.' Let's give M.I.T. a schoolin,' and reject their foolin', about the parking-lot surveillance thing.

6. Now, Citizens of Boston, please reclaim your heritage. Don't fall for every story you hear. If the plot sounds phony, just assume it's baloney -- and let the fiction writers have their career.

Will he ever return? Yup, Tsarnaev will return. We're taking back our country today. It'll be great to shake the hand, of the Chechen who was damned, and see him ride the MTA.

-- Melody, 1880's, please get a band to record this!

GENUINE WARNING: ALL OF PART 5 IS TRIGGERING.

Allies at Yalta
L to R: Churchill, FD Roosevelt, Josef Stalin, Photo: CarnegieEurope.eu

At the 1945 Yalta agreement, when Churchill and FDR gifted the state of Eastern Europe to Stalin (who knows why?) some of those people saw they would be in trouble under the Russians because of their collaboration with Germany. Australian whistle-blower Fiona Barnett says The International Refugee Organization was instrumental in bringing to Oz many Slavs, Ukrainians, Serbs, and East Europeans after WWII. Some of these folks, back in Poland, Lithuania, etc, were already **Luciferians** and the Nazi party attracted them into working for the Nazi's.

Peter Holoczak came in with Fiona's grandmother, pretending to be her spouse, to Engadine, NSW. Fiona mentions a corridor of Nazi immigrants (not Germans) settling all the way south from Sydney to Wollongong. Her main tormenter was Dr Leon Petrauskas. Fiona describes him as a Jesuit Luciferian. She claims that over time, the immigrant descendants of the Luciferian pedophiles collaborated with existing Luciferian dynasties and **infiltrated** Australian government and influenced law. I'll quote from her article at humans arefree.com and her book *Eyes Wide Open:*

"I was child-sex-trafficked to California in a cargo plane, having been gassed and **stuffed in a wooden crate like an animal.** I was trafficked to the annual summer camp at Bohemian Grove. I was one of a group of children dressed as teddy bears and **hunted for sport by men** to the theme song Teddy Bears Picnic and witnessed a ritual murder. Kim Beazley, Sr, a **parliamentary leader in the Labor Party, was the head of the trafficking operation.** Jim Rothstein, a New York Police detective, told me that the CIA were behind a blackmail operation in which **child prostitutes were used to honey-trap and compromise politicians,** military brass, top businessmen, and government officials.

"These are covens based on nationality (e.g., there's a strong Scottish coven in Bundaberg), sexual orientation (e.g., Bond University has a lesbian coven), gang membership (bikie gangs).

"It is from these lines that the cult obtains 'breeders' – women who are forced to breed unregistered babies for sacrifice and sex trafficking. Their behaviour is usually barbaric and requires constant management to stop them exposing the cult. **Child rape, torture, and murder are routinely practised within Luciferianism for various reasons.** These acts are established traditions thought to appease their god Lucifer. Killing kids **is believed to bestow power on the practitioner. Sodomy is called the 'fountain of youth' and is thought to transfer the child's youth to the abusing adult."** [All bolding today by MM]

In my opinion, Fiona is worth listening to, as her statements are backed up by other miscellaneous findings in the writings of such whistleblowers as Kathleen A Sullivan*, in Unshackled;* Cheryl Hersha (married name Cheryl Beck), in *Secret Weapons; and* Wendy Hoffman, in *Enslaved Queen* and *After Amnesia.* Barnett says:

"Luciferianism is a cult. Cult indoctrination alone is a strong enough influence on human behaviour. But the impact of indoctrination is reinforced by fear of the consequences of betraying or exposing the cult. **The number one rule of Luciferianism is – there is no such thing as Luciferianism.**"

Barnett thinks Mind control is a Luciferian tradition stemming back thousands of years. Luciferian offspring are trained in witchcraft and psychic manipulation of the physical elements. I can't verify that and Fiona is not a historian, but she is very valuable when telling of her personal experiences. For example, she says:

"Children are tested at age 3 for whether they should be raised with conscious or dissociated awareness of their cult involvement. [Mothers may well panic over that statement.]

"Children with a strong ethical objection to cult practises **are never made aware of their involvement.** These children are forced to dissociate through trauma, and their minds fragmented. My husband and I were two such children.

"There was an *Ordo Templis Orientis* themed ritual murder, with Antony Kidman and four others dressed in rather camp, coloured robes based on the Eastern Star pentagram which dominates the Alistair Crowley **Thelema** offshoots including Freemasonry."

Fiona has a copy of a document titled, International Camp, Oasis, and Lodge Master's Handbook, dated 2002. She says it lists the name **Kylie McKiernan as treasurer of the OTO**. Kylie was a senior person in Oz's ABC broadcasting network in 2015. In that year, Fiona reported her story to the Royal Commission, who mainly ignored it. But she did receive a payment under NSW Victims' Compensation for abuse by her grandfather.

Fiona mentions a link from OTO to a South-East Queensland DOCS pedophile ring that police raided in the year 2000**. DOCS** [Department of Child Safety] staff were intentionally placing foster children with pedophiles who were 'pimping' the kids out.

"The Luciferian pedophiles have infiltrated all areas of Australian government, education, health and human services. They have control over the police, media, universities, **defence forces**, parliament, schools, health services, churches of all denominations, psychiatric hospitals. Hillsong church was founded for the sole purpose of procuring child trafficking victims and produce kiddie porn **snuff** films.

"I came forward to Bathurst police detectives after Tor Nielsen reported to police that **he saw 60 children ritually raped in the [Bathhurst City Hall] by NSW Police and Catholic priests** who worked at nearby St Stanislaus College. Multiple St Stanislaus pedophiles have since been convicted for ritual abuse crimes."

My book, *Deliverance*, which is about Pizzagate, presents the story of bioweapons research in Papua New Guinea. I think it included experiments with kuru, which is related to prions. Barnett offers:

"My abuser Leonas Petrausaks was an expert in sea creature poisons. He attended the Australian School of Pacific Administration, a cover for MK-Ultra activity, weaponised anthropology, and MK-Naomi bio-weapons research conducted in Papua New Guinea. he worked alongside notable MK-Ultra recruits Margaret Mead, and Hitler's bio-weapons scientist, Erich Traub. ... Antony Kidman returned to Australia in 1972 after years of work at St. Elizabeth's Hospital, Washington DC.

"Antony Kidman and Leonas Petrauskas were close associates of Dr **Harry Bailey** who was trained in **deep sleep** methods by MK-Ultra perpetrator Ewan Cameron. The CIA funded Bailey's MK-Ultra deep sleep project at Chelmsford Private Hospital. I was subjected to MK-Ultra procedures by Harry Bailey, in the presence of Kidman and Petrauskas, at Chelmsford in Sydney.

"John Gittinger was the CIA's head psychologist. He developed the test battery to assess potential CIA case managers and agents. **All top Australian military brass were Luciferians. Most Sydney University staff were**, too. Child victims were **sourced from Luciferian** covens, various cults, Boys Town, juvenile detention centres, **child protective services,** foster care.... "

Note: The book at hand started out as an attempt to help Pridgeon in his Brisbane trial that was to begin 7 June 2023. It therefore emphasizes the issue of the Family Court, not mind control, not Lucifer cults, etc. I am baffled by how those things relate to one another, or to Freemasonry, or to the CIA.

I speculate that most folks who are abusing kids get used in some way, by the authorities. Perhaps it's mainly connected to power; it can't be easy to run 8 billion members of the human species!

My best guess about "Lucifer" (aka Moloch) is that it's a trick by which people who want to do bad can justify it religiously.

21. Karen Wetmore Makes Accidental Discoveries

(L) Karen Wetmore's book, Surviving Evil (R) Karen Wetmore, b 1952, Photo: mkultrahistoryday.weebly.com

Among the many books about MK-Ultra written by survivors, this one is unique.

Karen Wetmore was not selected as a child to be trained in the way survivor Carol Rutz was (via a military parent). She was not born into a family where torture was already happening, as was Trish Fotheringham. She was not born into a cult as was David Shurter. She was not sold on the slave market as was Brice Taylor. There is no mention in Karen's book of any satanic activity.

It's about medical experimentation that Karen discovered from reading journals and sending Freedom of Information requests. Her biggest find was that Dr Robert Hyde, working in Boston, engaged in "terminal experiments" -- how to kill softly with drugs. Deaths at Vermont State Hospital **were one every other day**.

Karen lived with normal, caring parents but happened to be sent to a Mental Hospital at age 13 when she had a breakdown. Personnel at Vermont State Hospital, VHS, were already doing CIA experiments (since 1950) and they seized her. They loaded her up with experimental drugs, including LSD, and engaged in an effort to make her have permanent amnesia.

I deduce from Karen's story that the exciting work of the 1960s in finding chemical cures for mental illnesses was deceitful. Karen is an example of someone who was given various mental illnesses deliberately. I have to say it makes me wonder how common this procedure is -- think about that possibility! Karen later learned that Mom had made many attempted visits to VSH but was told that Karen did not want to see her.

(Flashback. Cherri Bonnie went to visit Martin Bryant in Risdon Prison Infirmary but was told he did not want to see her.)

Wetmore tells us that the main man doing experiments in Dachau concentration camps in WWII, Dr Hubertus Strughold, was allowed to come into US under Operation Paperclip. He worked at the Boston Psychic Hospital, aka Massachusetts Mental. (p 81) Aside: I think we can say there was continuity in the investigations of the mind going on between Germany and the US, and there must be a tie-in with Tavistock in the UK. I suspect that the CIA does not work for a particular country but for the globalists.

At some point, Karen was given electric shocks, at 30 times the correct dosage. This was only a supplement to the main plan which was to erase her memory. (p 76)

Flashback. The late Trish Fotheringham in Victoria BC, told me that twice in her adulthood she accidentally discovered a talent that she must have trained at, under someone's control, but which she had no awareness of. The first was horses. A friend offered her the chance to ride a 'difficult' horse. She got into the saddle and had perfect control of the horse. The second thing was guns. Friends took Trish to a shooting range. She got the first try wrong, but after that it was bullseye every time. Same with Karen Wetmore -- she was offered the chance to shoot a Pepsi bottle and did it so well the bottle never even moved. Her pals were startled, and so was she.
It appears that Karen's memory loss was achieved chemically. Here is just one "dish" of medicines she took (p 50):

"The 1965 medical records [of Mary Fletcher Hospital] show that I was prescribed the phenothiazine drugs Thorazine and Stelazine. Over the next 30 days, I was also given frequent large doses of Sodium Amytal ["truth serum"] used in MKULTRA in a way to allow the researchers to map the subject's unconscious mind so the subject could be successfully exploited later."

One of the reactions Karen had to being overmedicated was the condition known as dystonia where your neck, or other body parts, goes into spasms. She also had two heart attacks and an autoimmune disease. Even when it became policy not to use those drugs, Karen was still subjected to them. She almost certainly was given the hallucinogen LSD, too. And during an EEG she was loaded with Metrazol which almost finished her off.

I want to state emphatically, from my studies of the CIA (or whoever poses as CIA), that there are no lengths of cruelty to which they won't go, when "competing" with a defiant citizen, or one who might spill beans. In the following instance, I think the motive was to stop Karen from leaving their care as she was a valuable experimentee. At age 17, she fell in love with 18-year-old Phil Cam (to whom her book, *Surviving Evil*, is dedicated) and they were about to elope. (p 60):

"Monday, August 4. 1969, was a rainy summer day.... I knew something was wrong and I called his house. His sister-in-law told me that Phil was in an accident.... I watched as my father whispered something to my mother.... Phil was killed in a head-on car crash as he drove from Rutland to Brandon. He pulled out to pass the car in front of him when another car pulled onto the highway. Phil couldn't stop."

Flashback. That happened to me, too, in 2021 in New Hampshire. I was in the front passenger seat. For no reason, a truck in the opposite carriageway came out of his lane and headed straight to us. My driver was very quick and swerved onto the shoulder of the road, so we only got car damage, no injury. If I'm correct that the offending driver meant to harm us, it could be that he is "on the payroll," but it also could be that his car was remote-controlled to do it. I doubt he had any motive to injure himself.

Note: I could be wrong, of course, but that trucker had no hope of passing. We were on a small, crowded street.

As for Phil Cam, if it was murder, there is no statute of limitations on that, and Vermont police can still delve into it. I hope they do.

Gang Stalking and Escapes

In other instances, Karen Wetmore was stalked, and occasionally gang-stalked. You can find an example of gang-stalking recorded in court by Patrick Knowlton, in connection with the murder of Clinton colleague Vince Foster.

Flashback: I have been with the late Blanche Chavoustie (a survivor) a couple of times when she was rather hilariously gang-stalked. She believed the purpose was to keep her generally aware that she had no freedom or privacy.

When reviewing her many hospitalizations, Karen figured out that her various **escapes** were probably "arranged." (pp 98-103). She was never stopped when running out the door. She was usually brought back by state troopers, whom she says treated her very respectfully:

"I believe that my escapes involved the use of triggered response mechanism set up in me by hypnosis and implants." (p 111)

Flashback: Did no one notice, when MLK was assassinated and it was blamed on a patsy, James Earl Ray, that Ray had been a fugitive from a prison? He had escaped by hiding in a bakery truck that regularly arrived at the prison before dawn.

The same is true of the alleged bomber of the 1992 Atlanta Olympics, Eric Rudolph. He managed to defeat all FBI searches for him for 5 years. I wager he was being held somewhere, or allowed temporary freedom, until he might be needed as a patsy.

Klaus Schwab

Now here is a eureka from "Surviving Evil" that may be relevant for the current World Order plan to a new system in which Klaus Schwab says "People will own nothing and they will be happy." Here Colin Ross is quoting from an MK-Ultra Subproject 49 document that discusses the CIA's interest in hypnosis (p 129):

"In order to investigate the possibility of hypnotic induction of unwilling subjects… [Don't you love it?] Can an **auto-hypnosis be taught so as to be as effective in the cancelling out of pain** or other stress conditions? A person could create his own world and be happy in it even though he was confined in a very small space which was extremely filthy."

The Blame Game and the Apology

While Ms Wetmore does often say that she is angry at VHS, and that she grieves for her lost life (as does Wendy Hoffman who was nearly 70 when she got the real story), the blame is largely on those who were not the guilty parties but who wouldn't part with information. I won't list them now. She filed a lawsuit in 1997 and was tricked by her own lawyer into settling in a way that prevents her going further now that she has more evidence.

No one in authority has ever acknowledged Karen's suffering. She did have many kind nurses and a few good doctors. Her best psychologist was Kathy Judge. A trusted doctor, Tom Fox, died of pancreatic cancer (p 44) which I consider to be a likely murder, and a beloved nurse, Cheryl, was found murdered, with no one charged.

However, there was a happy experience. A Social Security officer, who did not give his name, must have seen her records before she did. He came to her house and said — which she did not understand at the time: "I want to extend an apology to you from the entire state of Vermont."

There's much more in her book, *Surviving Evil.* Please get a copy.

Recap: Karen Wetmore was born in 1952 and first hospitalized in 1965, at age 13. The really bad stuff started in 1971 when she was experimented on by the CIA. She made umpteen attempts at suicide. Around 1997 she discovered what had been done to her. Unlike all the other survivor-authors, Karen did not learn about her past by dredging up a memory in therapy or by drawing pictures. She found it in hospital records, by persistence and luck.

Thank you, Karen. You have helped the world.

22. Was the Thalidomide Tragedy Intentional?

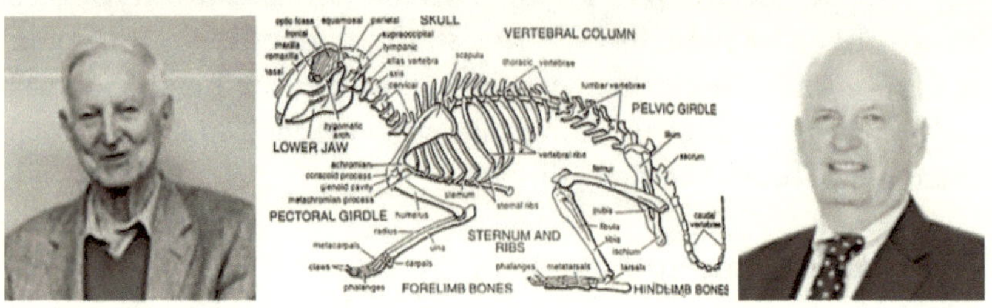

(L) Dr Bill McBride, Photo: Telegraph.co.uk (C) skeleton of a rabbit, Photo: disabledrabbits.com (R) Dr Doulas Keeping of Queensland

This chapter is not strictly related to the upcoming trial of Dr Pridgeon. A Gumshoe News Commenter complained that we had censored our own work on thalidomide. True, I did delete my 31 May 2021 article but re-run it now. It sheds odd light on the NSW Medical Council. For me as a law-trained person, one of the biggest discoveries about Pridgeon's case was the shadowy role that a Medical Council can play in cancelling a license.

I agree with Russell that such councils make it possible for the government to remove any doctor's registration -- good behavior no bar! And see, at GumshoeNews, my 2023 interview of William Sumner Scott, as to ABA's hidden power to punish a good lawyer.

Rabbits and Us. Here is my theory that the thalidomide tragedy was planned, as I discussed in my 2013 book *Consider the Lilies.* Thousands of babies were born without limbs. I had once read that experiments in the 1930s in Germany showed that one could prevent a rabbit's limbs from developing. This was done deliberately by tampering chemically with the embryo.

Thalidomide itself was not manufactured until 1957. Many animals, including humans, are tetrapods, that is, they have four limbs, and they are pentadactyls, that is, their limbs have five digits. It is known that limb buds form very early in the embryo. For humans, the limb buds for the child's arms appear early in pregnancy; leg limb buds soon after. It's known how the limb bud develops into a perfect limb. To name just two of the relevant substances, there is Fgf, fibroblast growth factor, and AER, apical ectodermal ridges. If, in the laboratory, you remove an animal's AER, the skeletal development of its limb will go astray.

(Since the 1990s, when gene mapping was available, one could switch off the growth of a limb by preventing the relevant genes from performing their task, but that post-dates thalidomide.) Note: Anyone who, in the 1950s, planned this event must have been born earlier than 1920 and so he/she is dead now.

Dr William McBride of Australia (1927-2018) In June 1961, two Sydney women gave birth to babies missing the upper arm bone. They were patients of obstetrician William McBride. When he delivered a third baby that looked just like those other two, he realized it must have been the morning-sickness pill he had prescribed: thalidomide. By 13 June 1961, he told the Australian distributor of the drug, Distillers Biochemical, about his suspicions. *They took no action.*

On the same day, McBride mailed a short article to *The Lancet.* To his amazement, a full MONTH later he got a rejection — as there was a large number of important (!) papers awaiting publication, said deputy editor, Dr I Douglas-Wilson. (In his book, *Killing the Messenger*, McBride says he could hardly bring himself to show the letter of rejection to his wife Patricia, herself a doctor.)

By September 4, McBride had delivered a fourth baby that was missing its radius. Two weeks later he told Wellcome pharmacologist Roland Thorp his theory: that deformities were produced by thalidomide. Thorp disagreed. On September 20, *The Lancet*, perhaps tipped off by Thorp, wrote an editorial saying that drugs taken by pregnant women may enter and upset the fetus. "It behooves all who care to be on the alert for it." [Do I detect sarcastic language?] However, the specific drug "thalidomide" was not mentioned!

If you read McBride's book, *Killing the Messenger,* and Harold Evans' book, *The Paper Chase,* you may agree that the behavior of the manufacturer is a give-away. Pharma normally responds with alacrity to complaints, for fear of lawsuits. But here, silence was resolutely maintained. I say this was done **in order to make time** for more mothers to take thalidomide. (Look how the CDC pushes for children to take a Covid vaccine today -- ***after*** its dangers have been demonstrated.)

The Manufacturer. Chemie-Grunenthal is a post-war pharmaceutical company in Aachen, Germany, continually owned by the family of Hermann Wirtz. They marketed a drug called Contergan, which we call thalidomide. It was a sleeping pill, or tranquilizer for adults, and an antidote to morning sickness for pregnant women The drug, when first sold in 1957, caused neurological damage in adults, and in embryos it caused a range of malformities, particularly birth of children without full arms and legs.

The main country affected was Germany, in 1960 and 1961, with thousands of such children. Many were stillborn, or died, or were allowed to die (I think they means they were not fed). The UK had the second largest group. Australia and New Zealand together had about 100 affected children. The US did not have casualties, as the drug had not obtained FDA-approval there.. By 28 November 1961, it was withdrawn from all markets.

A Criminal Case was brought against Grunenthal in 1968, but no one was either convicted or acquitted. It must have been for negligence as no one has ever said the manufacturer did harm deliberately. Per the *New York Times*, on December 18, 1970: "ALSDORF. West Germany's thalidomide trial was discontinued today after two and a half years under a compromise settlement providing some compensation for those who are believed to have been victims of the sedative. No formal verdict was pronounced against the defendants, five employees Of Chemie Grunenthal.

But the Aachen District Court declared that it held thalidomide responsible for the birth defects of thousands of West German infants and for the nervous disorders that about 800 adults suffered." In December 2013, at the Victorian Supreme Court, a class action by the Australian and NZ survivors resulted in a pay-out of $81 million AUD for 100 claimants, $810,000 per person.

A Hero and a Target. Now back to the Australian connection. In 2011, I published a congratulatory letter, on the 50th anniversary of McBride's discovery of the cause of the children's deformities. McBride's daughter told me that he wept when she read it to him over the phone. Why so? He had been hailed as a hero at first, and was made a Companion of the British Empire. The government of France gave him a huge award with which to set up an Institute in Sydney. But subsequently he became a medical pariah. McBride acted as an expert witness against another company, regarding the drug Debendox. That did him in — he had to be attacked. I said the following in my book *Consider the Lilies:*

"The subsequent persecution of Bill McBride should clinch it for anyone. This doctor was subjected to exactly the same (probably scripted by the exact same person) routine as was Andy Wakefield in regard to autism.... A combination of the New South Wales medical licencing board and Australian Broadcasting Corp did it.

"For Wakefield, it was media, especially Brian Deer, plus the General Medical Council.) An irrelevant matter was brought up against McBride – that he had performed 44 unnecessary Caesarians. A court case ensued for *years*, during which no patient had anything bad to say about him. Norman Swan of ABC accused McBride of fraud in research, having to do with rabbit's drinking water. The only doctor who could vouch for McBride in this rabbit-water matter, Jan Langham in the US, had just died, young."

In my opinion, the death of Dr Langham, should be investigated.

Portfolio-Shuffling in Germany. Now flash back to the trial of Grunenthal in Aachen, Germany in 1968, over the "Contergan scandal." Recall that the trial had "closed down" in 1970. There's no way certain persons were going to allow certain persons to be punished, right? But the problem couldn't just fade out, as the subject matter was painfully visible. Plenty of young Germans --

then around age 7 -- had to be in wheelchairs for lack of legs or had to acquire some amazing skills to make up for arm-lessness.

A 2014 article in *The Guardian,* by the late Harold Evans, points out that **the court made the decision to close the case** (!) and that the prosecution agreed. Evans wrote:

"The nine men charged with intent to commit bodily harm and involuntary manslaughter went free. The judges said this was with the explicit approval of the prosecution. They granted Grünenthal immunity from any further criminal proceedings.

"On July 21, 1969, the documents show, Grünenthal directors and their lawyers met in secret with the federal health ministry…On 18 September, four federal ministries were involved in discussing an 'overall solution,' meaning a high-level political intervention to stop the trial."

Natch. But who is this agreeable **prosecutor**? It is Dr Joseph Neuberger (1902-1977). the very man who, until shortly before, **had represented the defendant, Hermann Wirtz**, the founder of Chemie-Grunenthal (which had always been a family firm).

How could he become a prosecutor? Probably there was a change of Cabinet was for the purpose of shutting down the court case. It's easy to do when you own all Parties. Evans reports:

"There was a political coup that led to an SPD/FDP coalition. Neuberger (SPD) got the job of minister of justice for North Rhine-Westphalia, a post he held from 1966-1972. Three days before he took office, he wrote to the prosecutors to demand they stop proceedings against his client: 'I would be personally obliged for a rapid execution'." -- at *The Guardian.*

My Speculation about the FDA Connection. Around 1962, the FDA (US Food and Drug Administration) was given huge kudos for having refused to approve of the drug Kevodan (the

US name for the thalidomide pills). President John Kennedy gave a top award to Frances Kelsey, the officer in charge of the FDA. The narrative of the day was that Kelsey did not think enough research had been done. "Her caution saved us."

That strikes me as odd. The drug had been selling well in Europe for 3 years, and the US had no awareness that children were getting deformed by it. McBride's work persuades me of conspiracy. Imagine *The Lancet* not accepting a warning from an obstetrician who saw it happening in his own practice.! The way he was treated later, too, is weird. Note his obituary at abc.net.au is headlined:

"Dr William McBride: The flawed character credited with linking thalidomide to birth defects". That needs to be corrected. The flawed characters were the ones who made a four-year sport of harassing him in the dock. Like Pridgeon, a good doctor. How dare they call him a "flawed character"!

I carry my wild speculation to the point of imagining that the *main* purpose of the thalidomide tragedy was to create an aura of great respectability around the FDA. It did have that effect.

Perhaps the scandal of Covid today will put paid to FDA's authority. The FDA jumped to grant "EUAs" – emergency use authorization — for Covid vaccinations, when there is no emergency at all. The entire technology of the Moderna vaccine is new – so how can anyone give it approval with no animal testing?

By the way, I do not think the FDA legislation gives it anything beyond the task of determining the purity of foods and drug items offered for sale. There is no constitutional role for it to play in directing a doctor's work. Correct me if I'm wrong.

One Happy Aside. One doc, said that McBride's obstetric procedures were "well within the tram lines." Dr Keeping also said, in the witness box, that the case was "without substance" and was "a persecution." Thanks for helping Bill McBride, Doug.

23. Family Court Is Lethal. Now Will You Believe Me?

(L) Rat poison, Photo: automatictrap.com (R) Apple pie, Photo: Banquet.com

A lawsuit in the US District Court of Eastern Missouri will be a turning point, I hope. The alleged misdeeds of a GAL: *Guardian ad Litem* were so egregious that no one can excuse them. In June 2023 it was ruled that the GAL may not have immunity.

I offer you a brief review of the lawsuit that has been filed, by zeroing in on the main parts. I make no claim that the Plaintiff's statements are correct. Initial pleadings in litigation consist of unverified statements. The burden of proof is on the Plaintiff. However, the exhibits, such as doctor's letters and recordings of the children, do appear to back this Plaintiff up.

She, Cindy Haynes, has demanded a jury trial. She is the mother of four girls, one of whom hung herself on November 24, 2018. Cindy is suing G.A.L. Jennifer **Williams** (and some others but I will focus on the GAL). The sad/bad guy is her **ex-husband, Charles Haynes**. Upon marriage in 2008, mum already had two daughters, of which one, **MSH,** became a sex victim of Charles.

Together, the couple had two more girls, the now-deceased daughter, **MH**, and a younger one called **SH** who does not figure much in the story. **Grandmother** Bernice Haynes comes into the story as she, like her son, is a **Defendant**. At age 89 she got custody of NH and SH, from the Divorce Court.

Cindy Haynes v Jennifer Williams Case number 1:21-CV-00160-SNL. It was filed in November 2021. I'll list the **issues** according to my own 'schedule,' and base them on Gumshoe News' five years' worth of reporting and identifying the horrors of Family Law in Australia. Please read:

Issue A. What in the world **could have motivated the GAL** to do so many cruel things to the mother and the kids? Or to put it another way -- who paid or pressured the GAL to break many rules that attorneys are bound to obey? Was it the law firm she worked for? Was it the Judge in the Divorce case, Judge John Shock? Did she learn it in law school? Did the mafia put a horse's head in her bed? There has got to be a reason!

Issue B. What in the world brought legislatures in democratic countries to chip away at parents' rights to the extent that, if a parent is seen as having neglected the child's education, the state can take the kids away permanently? (Is THAT going to make him or her educated?) And, into the bargain, the state allows this to happen with no investigation. The Mom can show that her kid has practically earned a PhD in physics at age 12, yet it will fall on deaf ears if a GAL has said she noticed some "educational neglect." Zheesh!

Issue C. How in God's Name does a judiciary allow a case to run on and on? Here there were two cases bearing down on the plaintiff. One was the fact that in December 2013, Charles had been charged with the crime of sodomizing his stepchild, MSH. Yet he was out on bail during the three years covered in this lawsuit, always menacing the other sisters. Police already had Charles' admission on file, so what was anybody waiting for?
(I think I know. Do you?)

Issue D. Simultaneously, the divorce case was pending. Why should it take so long? All 50 states of the US now have No Fault divorce. That leaves two issues for a court to sort out if the parties don't agree -- money and kids' custody. And really, shouldn't the issue of custody be handled by a court that is experienced and fair on this delicate issue? The late Prof Freda Briggs recommended that any issue of *child abuse* be handled by an Inquisitorial court, not an adversarial one. I agree!

Issue E. How in God's Name did it come to pass that a job called GAL, or in Australia, ICL -- Independent Children's Lawyer -- would be assigned to a person (maybe not every time) that

followed some hidden rule known as Screw the Mother? Or, in this Missouri case, Screw the Child? In 2018, when Dee McLachlan conducted a survey of mums who had had a lousy time in court, her statistics showed that while many people believed the kids' story of abuse (doctors, teachers, aunts, etc), the ICL's consistently doubted the kid. As did also the court-appointed child psychologists. As did, I hate to tell you, the judge.
Kee-rist, who is paying the piper around here?

Now for this lawsuit, *Cynthia Haynes v Jennifer Williams*:

1. The GAL operated very unethically by being the attorney for Charles in the divorce case while also being the kid's attorney.

2. In those two roles she demonstrated her loyalty to Charles, and ignored, or worse, the kids.

3. She somehow got appointed by the court as the girl MH's actual attorney with the right to decide whether she could be hospitalized and, if so, who could see the records (not their mom) and who could visit them (not their mom).

4. She always let the kids know that she would recommend, in Charles' criminal trial, that he be given probation. (That did not happen, he pleaded guilty was sentenced to 7 years in 2018.)

5. Doctors (the ones in this story have got integrity, yipee) told GAL Williams that MH was suffering, such as cutting herself, out of fear of being raped by Dad. Yet she did not pass this on.

6. The bureaucracies don't come across too bad in this Missouri case (I know they do in some other states). Indeed, Family Service Department intervened to help the kids, yipee!), but they did not go far as to ask for punishment for the wrongdoers.

7. The kids were placed, together, in two foster homes, which meant a change of schools and being bullied as "whores" by classmates. But then they got into the foster home of Mr and Mrs Rideout, who did all good things, yipee!

8. Eventually, the kids were restored to Mom's home. Oh, and while they were at Grandma's, the kids said Grandma tried to kill Mom by sending her an apple pie with rat poison in it. But GAL told the kids not to tattle (Seppo for 'dob').

9. Constantly, GAL told the kids that if they spoke badly about Dad she would see to it that they got no more visits with Mom.

10. GAL similarly threated Mon constantly with an end to visits if she reported this or that to authorities.

11. Finally, two days before Charles' trial, 14-year-old MH committed suicide, apparently out of fear that Dad would go free and rape her. (The doctors think he was already raping her, though she never said so.)

Issue F. I can't be glad that the girl died, but since she did die, I'm pleased and relieved that this has turned into a lawsuit against a GAL. The Plaintiff is trying to make the Defendant pay damages under a Wrongful Death Act. This is not as difficult as trying to prove that someone criminally caused a death.

I sure hope the case gets publicity for the sake of the many protective parents who have a hard time letting their neighbors know that a GAL, or in Oz an ICL, does not in any way live up to the dream of speaking on the child's behalf. In Australia the ICL usually never meets the kid.

Issue G. But where is the judge? In Missouri, judges are elected, not appointed. Oh dear, this raises the specter of rigged elections. Yet even if Judge John Shock's election, in 2014, was as kosher as you can get, who was he to let such outrages occur in his court? Blind Judge Freddy can see that a GAL's persistent reference to a mother's educational neglect, and nonconcern for anything else, is a bit peculiar. Seriously, who is he answering to?

Issue H. Um. Where is the disciplining of a runaway GAL? Her colleagues in court, and her bosses at the law firm (who also are Defendants in Plaintiff's suit) can't be unaware of her behavior.

Everyone at the Divorce Court must know that she has an almighty conflict of interest, being on the side of Charles, while also being the attorney for the kid. Is there an ethics board?

Issue DAD. Whatever else is going on (and I, for one, find it all quite hard to understand), there is the question: How did Charles get to be such a rough guy? A part of the lawsuit that I find quite informative deserves some space here. It is about cycles of abuse. I am quoting Paragraphs 23 to 34 of the pleadings:

23. During Plaintiff's marriage with Charles, Plaintiff and her daughters struggled through cycles of Charles' abuse. The verbal abuse started early in the marriage, with Charles often calling Plaintiff "stupid bitch," "stupid Bible thumper," "whore," and "dumb and lazy bitch, who deserves to die."

24. [He] abused his daughters, and his stepdaughters, physically and emotionally during his cycles of abuse. He referred to his daughters and stepdaughters as "stupid," "worthless bitches," "dumb bitches," "failure," "queer," "freak," and "sluts and cunts, just like your mother" often outside [her] presence.

25. Generally, the first phase of an abuse cycle is the "honeymoon phase," where the abuser creates a safe place filled with love and a sense of security in the relationship. The victim is drawn close to the abuser by a powerful sense of belonging.

26. The second phase of the abuse cycle is the "tension building phase," when the victim becomes aware of the tension increasing in the relationship. The abuser uses a variety of techniques to maintain control over the victim, such as the silent treatment, jealousy, mind games, blaming, and gaslighting. The victim tries to appease the abuser in order to decrease the tension.

27. The third phase of the abuse cycle is when the abuse is exposed or the abuser feels a loss of control. This "explosive phase" begins when victim becomes target of extreme verbal, emotional, and/or sexual abuse at the whim of the abuser.

28. Charles repeatedly cycled through all three phases of abuse.

29. Plaintiff was naïve to the fact that she was a victim of domestic and intimate partner violence as she dutifully and lovingly met her daughters' needs for emotional support, loving parenting, and access to appropriate medical and mental health treatment even while Charles was abusing all family members....

32. On May 7, 2011 Charles assaulted Plaintiff at their home. Plaintiff heard Charles screaming at his stepdaughter, M.S.H., who was playing with her friend in her bedroom with Barbie dolls. Charles demanded that M.S.H. open Barbie doll's legs "to do some nasty!" When M.S.H. refused "to do the nasty," Charles started yelling and screaming at M.S.H.

33. Plaintiff rushed into the bedroom and asked Charles to leave M.S.H.'s room. Instead, Charles assaulted Plaintiff by punching her face breaking her nose and cheek bone in front of M.S.H. and her friend. Plaintiff, bleeding profusely and suffering a terrible headache, rushed to the Southeast Health Center of Ripley County where she was hospitalized and treated for her injuries.

34. Plaintiff filed for divorce, but then Charles immediately transitioned into the "honeymoon phase." He begged Plaintiff to forgive him because he was "a changed man" who would never again hurt Plaintiff and [the girls]. In reliance on these promises, Plaintiff naively dismissed her divorce with Charles.

Comment by MM -- It'll be easy to follow this case on Internet. Case number **1:21-CV-00160-SNL.** I recommend that every law school in Australia require the students to write an essay as to their personal reaction on this kind of behavior coming from their chosen profession. And then write up a list of any criminal charges that may flow from what is reported in this case.

It is a big breakthrough that the judge did not dismiss the case on the grounds that a GAL has 'immunity.' My guess is that Defendants will settle the case privately rather than face Discovery. And the bad guys would be dreading spillover to similar cases!

24. Hands across the Ocean and Mind Control

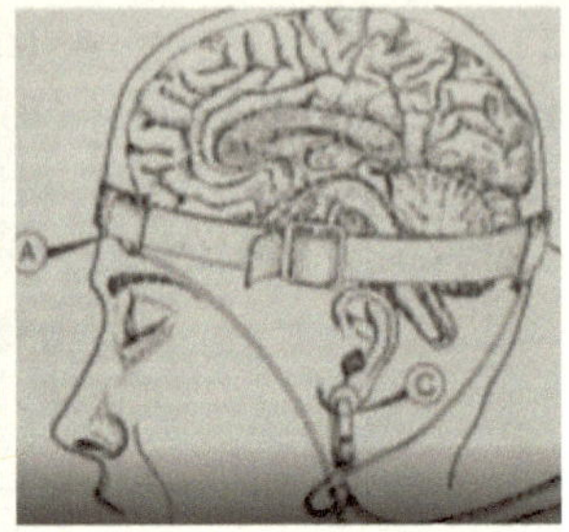

(L) Aztec ceremony of heart-removal, Photo: Wikipedia (C) Sarah Moore, Photo: distractify.com (R) Deep sleep, Photo: Flickr at piac.asn.au

Since 2005, I have known about extreme child abuse, thanks to Carol Rutz. She spoke at a meeting in Connecticut, under the auspices of Neil Brick at SMART, which has hosted survivor's conferences since 1998. After then reading Rutz's book, "A Nation Betrayed," I read Kathleen A Sullivan's "Unshackled," and this prompted me to run for Congress in 2006 from the state of New Hampshire.

The goal of this chapter is twofold: to show how the Internet enables persons with a grievance in one country to get help from abroad, and to make an outline of child sexual abuse.

Hands Across the Ocean

The following picture of international connections is based merely on my story. I do not have a map, as such, of what is going on all over the place.

The very picture of "hands across the ocean" came to me yesterday when Diane DeVere, in Australia, linked Gumshoers to a video of Angela Power-Disney in Ireland, interviewing Sabine McNeill in Germany about her arrest in the UK. It was published by Dee McLachlan in Australia and read by me in US, under which I appended a video of Chris Steyn being interviewed by Marianne Thamm in South Africa.

Think of this: Were it not for the Internet, the trials and tribulations of, say, the South African group, or the Australian sufferers, would be known only within their own countries. Indeed, they may be known only to the sufferers and close family. The mainstream media was never doing much to publicize such things. Note: I realize that some of the abuse is not systematized -- my personal history is skewed. The Rutz and Sullivan books brought me straight into the MK-Ultra area, and from 2005 till 2015, I was mainly studying the **mind-control** aspects of child abuse. Since 2018, Dee McLachlan has drawn me into the court-based aspect whereby judges participate in child-trafficking.

Categorizing Child Abuse

Now I would like to do some sorting. The book at hand is roughly based on the book by Russell Pridgeon, a doctor in Australia whose 'crime' is that of helping two children escape from abuse. Since the reported abuser of those kids happens to be their legal, biological father, I guess it can be categorized as **incest.**

I don't know if that man is connected to a **racket**. It appears that the authorities have shielded that man in a way that implies "connectivity." When mandatory reporters, such as teachers and doctors, hand in a report about the child's disclosures, the cops hide those reports rather than act on them. Why does this happen?

My Categories

I label the following as "my" categories, only in that they got to be that way, in my head, via my experiences. I suppose many other people see the categories in a similar way. Note: I must inevitably delve into the matter of mind control here.

#1. The **MK-Ultra** story. It is not a secret that Allen Dulles, who later became the first head of the CIA in 1948 (and whose brother John became US Sec'y of State in 1953) was interested in training children to do unconsciously what was commanded of them. I don't mean he didn't care to do it to adults also, but here we are talking about children. MK-Ultra work was contracted out to universities and hospitals and involved, quite simply, torture.

Why didn't the kid report it? She did not know it happened — that's part of the deal. But much later they remembered it — as with Carol Rutz and Brice Taylor. Why didn't the torturers report it? I don't know. I wish they would come out of the woodwork. Svali has done so, and asked forgiveness. (She was a victim who was forced to torture others, as is often the case.)

#2. The Kay Griggs story. Kay was married to a high-ranking military man who, when drunk, told her some secrets about "**the cherry Marines**." An eight-hour interview of her, by Pastor Strawcutter, has been on YouTube for years. Kay is very credible. According to her, Henry Kissinger controlled a group of men by raping them. It may be that sexual intimacy among males causes a bonding that the makes them cooperate in any tasks for the group. This could also explain the Yale-based Skull & Bones fraternity. Guys who are invited to join it in their senior year have a sexual initiation making all of them seem like a sort of mafia.

#3. Medical experimentation. Everybody knows that **Dr Josef Mengele** performed medical experiments on prisoners in the Nazi concentration camps, whether involving teeth or nutrition or the mind. He was not a lone wolf; there had been experiments in German since 1880 or so. Mengele himself, contrary to the US government story, did not die in Germany or retire to South America. He participated in the US, UK, and Canada in MK-Ultra stuff. Wendy Hoffman of New York tell of this in her book "Enslaved Queen." I believe her, and Carol Rutz also was treated by "Dr Green" -- an alias for Mengele. By the way, Mengele's doctorate was in anthropology, not medicine.

#4. Relatedly, there is **Tavistock** in the UK whose website describes it as a charity. In Australia we know of Tavistock in connection with Martin Bryant who was used as a patsy for the Port Arthur massacre in 1996, which often happens. (Has been in prison in Tasmania all these years but is innocent. God forgive us.) Dr Cunningham Dax of "Tavi" was his psychiatrist.

Diane DeVere reports that her grandmother in the 1940s was tasked with bringing Tavistock, to Australia so that **Australia would become the headquarters of mind control**. Nodes of Tavi were set up in Townsville, Qld, Ballarat and Geelong, VIC.

#5. Speaking of Dr Dax, he founded the University of Melbourne's Department of **Psychiatry**. I think the general idea was to make psychiatry an academic-based discipline. It is possible, but I have no particular evidence, that the mental health field is a subsidiary of the mind control field. At least in the cases we have seen of Child Protection Services, care for the kid's mind and emotions is not part of the deal. Why would that be so?

#6. **Psychotropic drugs** made an exciting new field in the 1950s. It was said that insane asylums would soon be emptied out, as such psychoses as schizophrenia would be controlled by medication. At the same time, however, we had Aldous Huxley hinting that all people would lose their freedom but they would feel good. Yet at the same time, we heard that the Soviet Union punished dissidents not only by placing them in mental hospitals, but by making them experience this or that emotion (fear, anger, anxiety) with 'punitive' drugs.

#7. **Satanism** has some role to play in child abuse, although I cannot trace it to my satisfaction. Worship of Satan has been around since ancient times and it is being inserted into popular culture now, along with witchcraft. Offering a sacrifice to a god or a devil may involve the killing if an animal or a human. The Aztecs pulled men's hearts in pre-Columbian Mexico. Dutchman whistleblower, Ronald Bernard reported to the International Tribunal for Natural Justice a few years ago that he was recruited into a group of 8,000 bankers who ran the world's finance and was asked to cut up a baby. He refused.

Note: They "should have" bumped him off for that but he went free and later turned up as a whistleblower. There may be a million whistleblowers out there.)

#8. Many MK-Ultra survivors, such as Kathleen A Sullivan and Cheryl Hersh Beck, were raised in a Christian fundamentalist sect. Anne Moore of the Mormons, said that they attended **churches, usually in basements**, at which the rites included the sacrifice of a child on an altar. In the 1800s, a Sabbatian Jewish cult practised some sort of satanic religion in Europe. In Australia, Fiona

Barnett has claimed that she witnessed sacrifices in the great hall of University of Sydney, for which the audience was upper class.

#9. Also in Australia, there was **a cult** known as The Family. It was run by Anne Hamilton Byrne. She said she had adopted or given birth to 14 children, who then lived with her at Lake Eidon in rural Victoria. Cruelty was the order of the day. I am guessing it was an experiment organized from outside. One of Anne's children, Sarah Moore, grew up to be a physician, but died young after writing the revelatory book "Unseen, Unheard, Unknown."

Two odd factors were the presence of an Indian guru, and the involvement of a man who had been Australia's Governor General, Baron Richard Casey (1890-1976), that is, a vice-regal.

#10. A massive book by Joachim Hagopian, a West Point graduate now living in Bali, is entitled "Pedophilia and Empire," meaning the British Empire. Just think of the fact that a prime minister, **Edward Heath**, was never called to account for the apparently well-known fact that he would take boys out on a boat, use them, and drown them. Hagopian also records the absolute free rein that **Jimmy Savile** had over children-in-care, including at Broadmoor mental hospital, plus access to the royal family.

#17. We have the whole phenomenon of **Hollywood** as a controller of child stars. Corey Feldman has been trying to whistle-blow on this one, but most colleagues remain silent. Stanley Kubrick allegedly said show biz is pedophilia or something similar to that. I have not put any time into researching this. Dee McLachlan has recently come across the way Record Labels control stars, such as Madonna, and if one dares to leave, he or she gets killed.

Please see next page for 'The Fodder Note,' by anonymous. Unsigned it lacks "probative value in court. However, Martin Bryant is still alive, and could verify it! -- He has been wrongly imprisoned for 27 years -- perhaps just to keep a lid on all this. I think it sounds like ASIO or CIA authorship. Or Mossad. I am sorry that it may be too much for survivors to listen to. Please take care:

Martin Bryant "randomly picked" as secret services "child fodder", meeting 1988 Unley, South Australia, at his handlers' orders, chaperoned by [redacted] who introduced him as a 'cook', he wants to kill people and tried to paint him as worthless and disposable. He showed **no sign of mental incapacity**, psychiatric condition, retardation or PHTs. [Unsure of the term; maybe post-hypnotic something]

His body language indicated apprehension. We established that he had been drugged unconscious for the trip from Tasmania, following the usual – expressly forbidden – practice and injected with the usual antidote immediately before being ushered into our office. He was bewildered by the strange environment. We tried to allay his fears. His verbal communication was understandably reticent, but his body language quickly indicated a trusting, open nature.

Specifically questioned on the allegations of wanting to kill people, Mr Bryant was coherent, clearly denied, showed fear. We offered protection... but his handlers immediately rushed in and whisked him away. A few weeks later he was again brought to us. He could not walk unaided. **He had clearly been severely Electroshocked and overdosed on neuroleptics**, displaying an absent gaze, with an attention span of five seconds or less, constantly stooping head.... He was unable to recognize the interviewer, had lack of muscle coordination (e.g., **inability to close mouth and control flow of saliva**), and symptoms congruent with very heavy dosage of benzodiazepines. He had some uncontrollable jerking of limbs and body rigidity. His handlers [said] in his presence, and in very menacing tones, that they had "done it", that he was "gone", that they would kill him, and that we should take as proof of his worthlessness the state he was in and the symptoms which they declared to be epilepsy!

It was revealed the same treatment would be applied to **us** should we make any move to defend Martin or divulge.

Subsequent history has shown **their threats were not idle**. At a later date a staff from **Glenside** visited us and informed that Martin had been imprisoned incommunicado (and hypnotically induced). Similar follow-ups by former **Hillcrest** psychiatric staff. [Emphasis added]

#11. Next is the story of "The Lost **Boys of Bird Island.**" That is the name of a book co-written by a retired cop, Mark Minnie (now deceased — by 'suicide'!) and Chris Steyn. It says that on that island, a few of the very high ups including the Minister of Defense, Magnus Malan, abused boys and killed them. Note that even after the book's publication, with much documentation, no arrests have been made. It's hush hush.

#12. Child sex for cash. I categorize thus as **economic.** Kids get stolen like any other property. They are salable and rentable. There is a market for child pornography. Since some of the films are 'snuff films.' it seems that there is a market for voyeurism of death. Not the same as another market — for necrophiles, i.e., persons who want to have sex with dead bodies. There is also the Epstein-like industry of using child sex to blackmail men. I have heard, but am not ready to endorse, that children are also used for their blood, known as adrenochrome, a drink that makes adults get high. Since Dickens' day, kids are used for labor.

#13. My Canadian friend Trish Fotheringham, RIP, told me an interesting thing. At age 19 she got ejected from a sort of MK-Ultra situation which also involved intergenerational incest. Her grandfather was the perpetrator and when he died there may have been a lack of others to continue 'training" her. She was thrown out on the street having first been programmed to believe that she would only ever be a **drug addict and a social dropout**. She adopted that role, until someone enlightened her in her 30s. Maybe many of our dropouts are like that?

#14. Trish died before the full-on propaganda that encourages the **sexualization of children**. But she was furious about beauty pageants for 3-year-olds. She even hated to see little girls adopting woman-like poses in clothes modeling, such as for a K-Mart catalogue. In her own life she had been a lap dancer since age 3 and was taught how to be sexy. She says the government also sold the technique to the Mafia.

#15. Trish, like Brice Taylor, was a **demonstration model**. A group of customers would gather round and watch how effective her submission was and if customers signed up to buy the relevant mind-control technique they could put it to any use. Brice's audience were dentists attending their annual meeting in Anaheim CA. First, a much-less provocative demo was given. Dentists who asked the right questions were invited to a higher meeting. Further, the clear devotees were invited to the real demo.

#16. Canadian Anne Diamond, a survivor, is the author of "My Cold War." Many children of military men blame Dad for **letting them be experimented on** (whether for cash, or to win the dismissal of some criminal charge against them). She believes her father did it innocently. If I remember her other writings correctly, she named some names of popular singers who were cruel to her, including Leonard Cohen, composer of *Hallelujah.*

#18. Let's mention the odd thing known as **'deep sleep treatment.'** It killed many patients at Chelmsford Hospital in Sydney, and at Memorial Hospital in Montreal. The goal was to wipe out a person's mind. All your memories and training (such as how to play the piano or even how to walk) would be gone. A secondary goal was to then fill that empty mind with another person's mind -- perhaps by connecting the two brains by wire. Need I say, the plan failed. Some Canadians got compensation. The investigation in Australia went nowhere; Barry Hart was badly treated by all of us who did not come to his aid.

#19. Max McIntyre, father of Rachel Vaughan (see Chapter17), was a bodyman tasked with disposing of, say, persons killed by CIA. He identified with **Rosicrucians and other occult groups**. Kathleen A Sullivan's father also was a bodyman and taught her techniques of cutting up bodies and putting them in acid.

#20. Tunnels. Some cities, including London, openly admit that a century ago there was large array of tunnel under the street. This reminds me of the tunnels at McMartin pre-school and Presidio Base in California, whose existence is denied by government.

Note: Some survivors offer healing, e.g., Anneke Lucas, Anastasia Sprout. Jeanette Archer will host an SRA meeting in UK in 2023.

***End of Part Five: Evils* //** **Luke, Chapters 4 and 10**

A voice came from heaven "Thou art my beloved Son; in thee I am well pleased." And the devil said unto Jesus, "If thou be the Son of God, command this stone that it be made bread." And Jesus said, "It is written, that man shall not live by bread alone, but by every word of God."

And the devil, taking Jesus up into a high mountain, shewed unto him all the kingdoms of the world in a moment of time, and said "All this power will I give thee, if thou therefore wilt worship me." And Jesus answered, "Get thee behind me, Satan."...

On one occasion an expert in the law stood up to test Jesus. "Teacher," he asked, "what must I do to inherit eternal life?" "What is written in the Law?" he replied. "How do you read it?" He answered, "'Love the Lord your God with all your heart and with all your soul and with all your strength and with all your mind'; and, 'Love your neighbor as yourself'." But he wanted to justify himself, so he asked Jesus, "And who is my neighbor?"

In reply Jesus said: "A man was going down from Jerusalem to Jericho, when he was attacked by robbers. They stripped him of his clothes, beat him and went away, leaving him half dead. A priest happened to be going down the same road, and when he saw the man, he passed by on the other side. So too, a Levite, when he came to the place and saw him, passed by on the other side. But a Samaritan, as he traveled, came where the man was; and when he saw him, he took pity on him.

He went to him and bandaged his wounds, pouring on oil and wine. Then he put the man on his own donkey, brought him to an inn and took care of him. The next day he took out two denarii and gave them to the innkeeper. 'Look after him,' he said, 'and when I return, I will reimburse you for any extra expense.'

"Which of these three do you think was a neighbor to the man who fell into the hands of robbers?" The expert in the law replied, "The one who had mercy on him." Jesus told him, "Go and do likewise."

Magna Carta, Photo: Huntington Library Art Collection

Here in Part Six, the subject matter is "the future." I consider some things discussed earlier -- such as the turning upside down of the law -- to be on their way out. Humans are nothing if not intelligent and can recognize when they've gone off track.

As announced in Chapter 1, I look upon the book by Russell Pridgeon, entitled *Everybody Knows*, to be a liberating gift. Not that Russell has come up with a new theory of the human race, quite the contrary. He is old-school all the way. He understands that we had good arrangements in the past and he hopes to see them restored. I am pretty sure they will be restored.

Don't worry, I'll also entertain some new ideas before this book ends. But first let me list some achievements in law and human relations. I have stated them in previous works, such as my 2021 book *Keep the Republic, Kill the Takeover.* Some are pointedly Seppo, but the US got much of this from England. Basically, it goes back to the Golden Rule which is biological.

To recap what was said in Parts 1, 2, and 4 above, about Breakthrough, Law, and 'Kafka' there exists a solid body of law that folks are generally aware of and hope to invoke when in trouble.

So-called 'private law' sorts out disputes between two parties -- this includes contract law and torts, in other words lawsuits.

For 'public law,' which includes all of criminal law, the aggrieved party is the community. Hence, since O'Dea broke the law, his case is called The King v O'Dea. The Marathon bombing case is called United States v Tsarnaev. Governments prosecute crime.

Can you sue the government by private law? Yes, I've done it in two war-powers cases; *Maxwell v Bush* and *Maxwell v Trump*, and in a civil RICO action, *Maxwell v FBI et al.* Also I sought an injunction, which is private law, against mandatory vaccination in *Maxwell v Sec'y of Defense*, Sec'y of DHHS, et al. All these cases were dismissed for "lack of standing" -- an obstacle that can easily be removed, and should be removed now, by the legislature.

The other day I saw a video by Jordan Peterson who is a psychologist with a powerful intellect. He said (at age 61) that he recalls a time, not that long ago, when Canadian institutions could all be trusted -- including government. They were solid.

I was glad to hear it, as I was beginning to doubt myself. I had happily trusted our institutions (academia, for example) but now that they've ceased to inspire trust I wondered if I'd been wrong all along, sort of projecting goodness onto them. OK, I now think they *were* trustworthy but have fallen. Are they salvageable? Maybe, but only if their sins get confronted and corrected.

Cancel Immunity and Impunity

Let's start here, then. If the institution of government is to be salvaged, we must return to the idea of its members being accountable to the community. Why the hell shouldn't they be accountable? The fact that officials today clearly think they owe allegiance not to the public but to their little club is sufficient proof of wrongdoing. They have fallen off the rails.

Wait. I hear you say they did not go off the rails; they are on a different set of rails where they are thriving. No! No! We can't have one reality on the books (the law of the land) and another in which fancy people are playing a different game, and not admitting to it. Especially where their game is a full-scale attack on the law of the land.

A simple correction would be for us to cancel **immunity** and **impunity**. Government people do not have any legal immunity when they commit a crime. They do have legal immunity against lawsuits related to their work, but not for crimes. No one is above the law. They pretend to be immune, and they tell you they are immune but happily that is not true. The sovereign *state* does have immunity, but this can be gotten around. Trust me. (There are also immunities given to elicit cooperation; these seem OK.)

Impunity is a different creature. From the Latin *impunitas,* it means without punishment. That is the real problem. For years we have heard that Joe Biden got huge payments from the Chinese state, for no apparent reason. He enjoyed impunity -- our failure to investigate or punish -- both when the DoJ was Democrat controlled and Republican controlled. Similarly, we all act as if we can't touch the child-traffickers (such as the AFP). But we can!

But How To Control the Powerful?

Much of human history involves people forcing their will(s) on others. In many of the competitions, *within* a society, the winner won by weapons, by guile, by royal inheritance, by charismatic personality, or by offering something that people needed. There is always some control from the top. Try setting up a commune where everyone-is-equal -- it won't stay that way for long.

When the competition is between groups, the winner is usually the side with the bigger population or the smartest technology. Genocide of the losing group by the winners is commonplace. I personally do not have a clue how to prevent "conquest." Here in I'll address only domestic control of the domestic powerful.

I mention the Golden Rule -- Do unto others.... Ordinary mentally healthy people know how to have social relationships. It includes refraining from ways to hurt or exploit the other. Nevertheless, there are individuals who lack the basic requirement of empathy, shame, guilt, or a sense of obligation such as to live up to agreements made. I have to suppose that, in regard to the evils listed in Part Five, many of the perpetrators are hopelessly mentally ill. They definitely shouldn't be tolerated as decision makers.

Legitimate Authority. Historically humans have a habit of finding ways to set up a government or a leadership, say of Elders. In pre-literate society people follow the leader. Once a person has acted as leader a few times it becomes natural to think he has some right to do so. He may claim to have special knowledge or access to magic. Humans are very prone to practice superstition.

By the time you or I came into the world, there were more sophisticated devices for conveying legitimacy. There was a big institutional government and comprehensive rules to obey. For a few centuries it had been the task of philosophers to figure out what legitimacy was. But now we best see legitimacy in the breach.

This whole book has been a tirade against the racket in which supposedly **legitimate office holders** steal children -- and punish anyone who gets in the way. Although we don't exactly know what makes them so industrious about child-stealing, we can easily see, that they make a mockery of everyone by breaking the law.

The Magna Carta, The US Constitution, and So Forth

Eight hundred and eight years ago, some English noblemen went to King John and coerced him to sign a charter laying out their rights. We could call it a power-sharing arrangement by persons who already had power, the barons, by wealth and family. They showed an understanding of law by pinning the king down to fulfillment of his legal duties. They even made him sign that if four barons had a complaint about King John, those 4 could gather 25 barons and, if necessary, distrain the king, and take his wealth.

Fast forward from 1215 to 1787. Fifty-five businessmen, more or less acting as delegates from the 13 states of the US, met in conference for 3 months (wearing velvet and wigs in a sweltering summer) to draw up a law that empowered the new federal government to do, and specifically not do, particular things.

Looking at that piece of parchment now, it is not obvious that the US would end up in its present condition of lawlessness, whereby officials enjoy impunity and citizens get treated illegally.

Two subsequent events enabled this. *1. Accumulations of wealth* threw out the function of fairly electing one's representatives to be lawmakers; corporations could see to it that their preferred candidate got in. *2. Fast development of science and technology* altered the social and cultural landscape, making surveillance possible and creating newly intimidating weapons such as Tasers.

The cultural changes included saturation by an unaccountable media. This could be used to design new family models, to load folks up with fears and hatreds, to distract with sports, and to create fictional 'realities.' By around 1950, education was not so concerned with teaching skills of reasoning. By the Year 2000, the value of truth was diminishing. Sinister forces, perhaps run by globalists with no national loyalty, dug in with restrictions on personal freedom and dignity. Seemingly anything might happen!

Maxims Are in Our Blood. The fact is that humans innately know right from wrong, since they can sense when the social arrangements are harsh and want to do something about it. Our common law contains broad principles known as *legal maxims*.

Maxims, from *Law Dictionary*, 1888, revised by Gilmer and Cox (arbitrary numbering added by MM; and Latin for my faves)

1. Acting and consenting parties are liable to the same punishment.
2. It is the duty of a good judge to enlarge his jurisdiction, i.e., to amplify the remedies of the law.
3. A good judge decides according to equity and right, and prefers equity to strict law. Bonus judex aequitatem stricto juri praefert.
4. A custom founded on a certain and reasonable ground supersedes the common law.
5. Crime vitiates all that springs from it. Crimen omnia ex se nata vitiat
6. Gross negligence is held equivalent to intentional wrong. Culpa lato dolo aequiparatur.
7. Let the punishment be proportioned to the crime.
8. False is one thing, false in all. Falsus in uno, falsus in omnibus.
9. He who flees judgment confesses his guilt.
10. Impossibility is an excuse at law. Impotentia exusat legem.

11. Impunity always invites to worse faults. Impunitas semper ad deteriora invitat.
12. We should judge by the laws, not precedents.
13. These are the precepts of the law: to live honorably, to hurt nobody, to render to everyone his due.
14. Necessity has no law. Necessitas non habet legem.
15. Law is the dictate of reason.
16. Law is a rule of right.
17. The law pays regard to equity.
18. The law will always furnish a remedy. Lex semper dabit remedium.
19. The law regards the course of nature.Lex spectat naturae ordinem.
20. The law assists minors. Lex succurrit minoribus.
21. An evil custom should be abolished.
22. Nothing is so opposed to consent as force and fear.
23. Too much subtlety in law is reprehensible. Nimia subtilitas in jure reprobatur.
24. He who cannot be known from himself may be known from his associates.
25. Odious and dishonest things are not to be presumed in law. Odiosa et in honesta non sunt in lege praesumenda.
26. He who acts through another, acts by or for himself.
27. He who does not disapprove approves. Qui non improbat approbat.
28. He who spares the guilty punishes the innocent. Qui parcit nocentibus, innocentes punit.
29. Let him be deceived who wishes to be deceived.
30. Where there are many counselors there is safety. Salus ubi multi consiliarii.
31. To write is to act. Scribere est agere.
32. Suppression of the truth is [equivalent to] false representation. Suppressio veri, expressio falsi.

A Negative Note about International Law. I think we are geared biologically for the sensibilities expressed in the maxims. But it applies only to a community in which we have relationships. I advise against trying to create global law as there is no one to enforce it. And who says we have to throw away our nations?

Reiner Feullmich had tried to take the Covid complaint to the ICC as a "crime against humanity." That can't work, but now he's going to the Maori's autonomous court in New Zealand. Yay!

26. King Charles, You Are Not "Authorized" in Australia

(L) Procession of the Knights of the Garter (R) Photo from Song album by Ted Egan in 1974

"Honi soit qui mal y pense" is the motto of the Order of the Garter, of which Charles III has now become the head. Other members of the Garter are John Major and Tony Blair. The motto is said to mean "Woe to anyone who thinks evil of us." Well, I think evil of them. I suspect that at Garter's HQ, mayhem is always on the drawing board.

I have just read that Charles planned to "slim down" his coronation ceremony," to dispense with some of the tradition." Understandably, he forsook the routine by which the monarch is made to go to the east, west north, and south of Westminster Abbey to get the "OK, we accept you" from the public. Hmm. That is or was the means of obtaining legitimacy.

What is legitimacy? If you act against the law, you are not being legitimate. Granted, the word is often used for something finnicky, like "Only this form of passport is legitimate." Or it simply invokes tradition, as in "The legitimate heir to the throne is 'X."

But in my claim here that Australia has no legitimate government today, I am thinking of the general collapse of law, and, separately, of the perfidy of Mother England (Gallipoli, anyone?). Either of those should cause us to face the fact that someone needs to grasp the nettle. Someone needs to get real and say Australia should no longer suffer a monarch.

My objection to a monarchy in Oz is that people do not understand that the monarch DOES rule Australia. For one thing he controls the removal of a bad judge (and he never does it). He also has full control over Parliament. No bill passes without the royal assent. Citizens may also charge, rightly, that the US and the Globalists run Oz. But it doesn't excuse the monarchy issue.

All six states could agree to cut the tie. Australia has been a nation since Federation in 1901. It is not tied to the UK by an enforceable contract. Indeed the federation of the states with one another is hardly enforceable. As none of the states are landlocked, states, they could go independent without having to obtain easements. Or they could marry NZ.

The Collapse of Law. At GumshoeNews.com we have, since June 2013, been airing the sad condition of law in Australia.

It is as though badness has the power to ruin anything, any institution. A big change is needed, with or without What's His Name, R. Allow me to enumerate 15 ways in which the government stands naked of law:

1. Famous episodes of violence were "False Flags" – e.g., Port Arthur, and the siege of the Lindt Cafe.

2. State police and federal police engage in crime — as seen in the Fitzgerald Inquiry of Queensland, or Denis Ryan's report of the protection given to pedo priests.

3. Prime ministers have sent Diggers to American wars, e.g., Vietnam and Afghanistan, for no valid reason.

4. The commonwealth government allows environmental harm – e.g., by fracking and pesticides.

5. Child Protective Services engage in sex-trafficking – as revealed through the Pridgeon, O'Dea, and Cling cases.

6. The premiers' Covid lockdowns were illegal — as seen in the use of a PCR, or the stopping of Serene Teffaha's class action suit against business losses during the Lockdown.

7. Parliament sells off society's property: Telstra and Qantas, and leases the Port of Darwin to China surreptitiously.

8. Doctors are told to obey politicians instead of science – as in Ivermectin, and Lyme disease.

9. Whistleblowers get harassed, such as Vaughan, McBride

10. Persecution of indigenous people continues, as in the land grab in Melville Bay and the cruelties at Dondale in the NT.

11. Tavistock or satanists get to practice mind control, as in Ballarat and Engadine.

12. Judges decline to apply the law, as in Muhamed Haneef's case or Fredrick Toben's case.

13. Australia acts as if it not entitled to protect its nationals, as in the case of Julian Assange, or the investigation of Aussie deaths in crash of Malaysian Airlines flight MH17.

14. Reports from public inquiries, such as Wood Royal Commission or the Mulligan Report, get placed under seal.

15. Australia yields its economy to a world government — as in the Lima Declaration or the WHO or the WEF.

Speaking of the WEF, when Charles was HRH Prince Charles, he assisted the Klaus Schwab's of this world in instituting a Great Reset, which we now recognize as including a genocide. If nothing else came into the problem of him becoming king of Australia, that would suffice. His leadership is to be rejected outright on grounds of the WEF factor.

I pass over the fact that his first wife Diana said that her husband was planning to have her removed via an automobile accident. Or that she said that Jimmy Savile was Prince Charles' mentor.

Note: the powerful like to say that Australians in 1998 rejected a chance, by referendum, to become a Republic. So what? That was a quarter century ago.

27. Would Invasion at the Border Justify a Mutiny?

(L) Border crisis, Photo: Nationalfile.com (R) Mike Prysner testifying at Winter Soldier 2008 meeting, YouTube.com

History is replete with rebellions by groups of men against their leaders. But probably not as replete as it should be! Rebelling is a hard thing to do. The deck is usually stacked against rebels. Where the group is small, it's easier for a few to plot the killing of a despised boss. Yet even there it may not happen. As noted in our own Declaration of Independence, "Experience hath shewn" that people will put up with a lot, rather than fight.

I suppose the ingredients for success are that a situation is intolerable, that the rebels have a way to communicate their plan in secret, and that they can envision what to do if it succeeds.

For purposes of this chapter, I'm inquiring about a mutiny, or some other kind of action within the US military, to counter the illegal border crossings that are taking place in huge numbers today. Thus, I'm not discussing action by cops or sheriffs in border towns, or the right of US citizens to keep invaders out. All of that is worth discussing, but my field is narrower.

I am looking only at rebellion within military service. I ask: What if the group crossing the southern border of the US were mostly fit-looking young men, army-like rather than a bunch of refugees. (This is genuinely hypothetical; I have no knowledge of it actually taking place.) If it were an invasion and did not evoke a US government response, could it justify a mutiny?

The Mutiny on the Bounty

In the old days, many a cruel sea captain manned a crew of fewer than 100 men. Why didn't the crew recognize the value of numbers and jump him? One problem aboard British ships, in the late 1700s, was that if a crew mutinied, the British Navy would still have the ability to find these rebels at sea and drag them home for court-martialing.

In 1789, Captain Bligh was treating his men badly on the *HMS Bounty* in the South Pacific. Also, Bligh seemed to be going off his rocker. Some officers on board were from the gentry (a career in the Navy being desirable for the upper class). One of them, Christian Fletcher, had the chutzpah to consult a few others on board about doing a mutiny.

They handcuffed Captain Bligh and pushed him into a smaller boat, rather than kill him, and gave him a few day's rations. Surprisingly, many men did not want to be rebels. They tried to get into the boat with Bligh and 20 of them succeeded. These were called Loyalists. Most of them made it to an island and eventually got back to England, with Bligh.

Fletcher took the *Bounty* to Tahiti and let many of the men disembark there. The rest went into hiding with him at the uninhabited Pitcairn Island along with 20 Polynesians whom they had kidnapped, including 14 women. Fletcher destroyed the ship so it would not be seen by other vessels. The men who got off at Tahiti were found in 1791 and three were hanged in UK. The group at Pitcairn raised families; their sons were young men when the mutineers were finally discovered by the Navy.

Now to the USA

I can think of many situations in the last century that could have instigated a mutiny in our military. I am not aware that any actually occurred, though they may have occurred and got hushed up. In the Vietnam war, circa 1969, there was quite a bit of fragging (soldiers who had been drafted, murdering an officer). It has not been the practice of US soldiers to rebel when asked to perform unsavory missions. The famous quote from US Marine General

Smedley Butler bespeaks a willingness of men to resign themselves to doing the dirty for their country. Or it reflects ignorance; Butler himself took a long time to get the gist:

"I spent 33 years ... in active military service and during that period I spent most of my time as a high-class muscle man for Big Business, Wall St, and the bankers. In short, I was a racketeer, a gangster for capitalism. I helped make Mexico and especially Tampico safe for American oil interests in 1914. I helped make Haiti and Cuba a decent place for the National City Bank boys to collect revenues in.... I brought light to the Dominican Republic for the American sugar interests in 1916. In China in 1927, I helped see to it that Standard Oil went on its way unmolested...."

It is a firm rule that all persons in the US military, from highest to lowest, must obey orders from the civilian government. Yet it should be noted that a private group, The Council on Foreign Relations, invites officers to join, and the Sec'y of Defense does not stop it. The CFR indoctrinates all its members into globalism. So how is it proper for generals to be in the CFR? John McManus has written a book about this, *Changing Commands.*

Lousy Conditions in the Military, and Opposition to War

Soldiers do frequently protest "conditions." Anti-anthrax shots in the 1991 Gulf War are possibly the cause of Gulf War Illness. The use of Depleted Uranium, DU, which has caused birth defect in children in Iraq, also harmed the US troops and their families. And, as seen in the testimony by many soldiers at the Winter Soldier conference, Army persons complained of their souls being messed up by being told to do wrongful things.

That reminds me of the fate of whistleblowers. I think Air Force woman Alyssa Peterson, although said to have shot herself, was more likely killed for using free speech, in complaining to her supervisor about the US torture at Abu Ghraib. You may recall that 12 generals signed a statement against torture (such as at Gitmo) -- but all 12 were by then retired. The younger ones may have had the same opinion but did not speak out. The Winter Soldier testifiers talked about their suffering and about their disagreeing with war policy. The whole point of Defense (unless you believe

Smedley Butler) is to defend one's nation. For this, it is logistically necessary that soldiers obey superiors, and that they go along with the war policy whether they approve of it or not. An army cannot be a democracy.

The Main Question Here. Today I am specifically inquiring about the issue of the southern border. Apparently, the Government has either issued a wrong policy -- it lets people enter the US who have not passed the requirements -- or the President is sneakily arranging for a sort of an invasion by hordes.

I am the author of a 2011 book, *Prosecution against Treason* -- it's aimed mainly at Congress. I think Congress is loaded with traitors to the US Constitution. But I would not put it past the Executive branch to go further, by inviting foreigners to enter the US to create mayhem. That would call for Americans in uniform to get involved even if the government forbids it. I mean if we had invaders, it would be crazy not to fight them off.

My stance is, and has been for a long time, that many things call for "mutiny" within any part of government. It is not morally correct to accept as "official" the actions of persons in government who, on paper, are working for this nation, but who, behind the scenes, are answering to someone else. Something must be done. Wake up! Don't say Ho hum!

Do We Want a Military Coup? About a year ago, there was talk of Gen Michel Flynn, perhaps supported by former US Attorney Sidney Powell, taking some direct action related to the 2020 Stolen Election. One story I heard (and I find it plausible) is that the then head of the CIA, Gina Haspel, was in Frankfurt Germany where some evidence about the steal was being held. The military broke in, took the goods, and then threatened to Gitmo-ize Ms Haspel unless she "sang." She sang.

If it's true, I conclude the emergency military intervention was legal. Consider how such a thing as an election-steal would have caused all our apparatus of the justice system to be silenced, if the stealer was now in office. After all, the president commands the FBI and could forestall any investigation of himself.

28. Workarounds Citizens Can Use To Reclaim the Law

-- *Google maps of New Zealand*

This chapter will argue that nothing as dramatic as a revolution, or marrying New Zealand, need be attempted. (By the way, NZ was invited to join Australia at Federation but declined to.) This doesn't mean that a citizenry can win against the powerful just by pointing to a few pages in a book, but we don't even try that!

First, note that many problems could be solved by government officials, but they choose to ignore the issues --trafficking, for example. Congress can investigate almost anything, but it does so only for 'local' reasons, such as competition between the major Parties. Any Member of Parliament can ask devastating questions at "Question Time," but disappointingly they do not do so.

Either they are ignorant of the issues or too timid to speak. Senator Rand Paul seems well informed and his father Rep Ron Paul was the only person to suggest that the US employ a little-known power to deal with Osama bin Laden, namely Letters of Marque, rather than start a war against Afghanistan over 9/11.

Another thing that we almost never see invoked is the Material Witness Act of 1792. This would allow the feds to imprison Bill Gates legally if he's said to be holding information about crime (sort of like Pridgeon being held with a tracker as a "flight risk.") He'd have no comeback such as "You're violating my civil rights," as the person can opt out of jail by coughing up the info.

One more underutilized area is a state nullifying an unconstitutional law. I only know of it being used by Kentucky and Virginia, in 1798! Richard Mack, former sheriff in Arizona says a sheriff in his/her county can semi-nullify by refusing to enforce bad law of state or feds, as SCOTUS agreed in *Printz v US* 1997.

And if your legislator is lazy, you can try taking his seat. I have tried it, but don't see how one can succeed against Big Money.

What a Lone Citizen Can Do. On your own, one way to act directly -- I don't mean by holding a protest sign, though that has some value -- is to sue the government person who is harming you. Also, you can legally perform a **citizen's arrest.** The requirements are that you know for sure that he has committed or is about to commit a felony, and that you tell him you are making a citizen's arrest, and why.

You may use force but if he can prove you wrongly arrested him, he can sue you for damages. Citizen's arrest rarely happens, as we are in the habit of depending on police. After you've captured the guy, you must invite the police to take custody of him.

There is also an unquestioned right of self-defense. If someone is coming at you, or at someone close by you, you may strike him and even use lethal force if necessary. By the way, I think **Wilfred Wong** was using this right as a means of rescuing an abused child. The media reported that he held the abuser at knifepoint. Cops had tracked Wong to the scene and he was arrested. An ex-barrister himself, Wong has not obtained justice.

A further law, from days of old, is the law of outlawry. Regular police did not exist until the 19th century. Before that, people depended on neighbor's help. Officially, if a person is uncatchable, he is said to be outside the law. He is an outlaw. Therefore, anyone can capture him or kill him. If you protect him such as by obtaining food for him, that is a crime. But check to see if your state or country has repealed the **common law of outlawry.**

Group Ways To Solve Issues of Negligent Government You can legally meet as a group and calling a TRC, Truth and Reconciliation Committee, or similar. Or form a citizen-led Grand Jury. If you see the government is not doing its job you can seek, in court, a Writ of Mandamus. In Australia, you can find mandamus at sec 75 of the Constitution. The US All Writs Act of 1789 grandfathered Mandamus in. It's codified at 20 USC 1651. (Google for any law, then choose the Cornell U explanation.)

Truth and Reconciliation. South Africa set the pace on this. In 1990, apartheid was dropped, and the question arose: how to deal with persons who had been cruel, especially the police. Note: in Russell Pridgeon's book *Everybody Knows*, he said that in his work in the 1980s in South Africa, he came home every day with his clothes covered in blood, as so many of the black patients he treated had been shot at, by police, for no reason.

I believe the question of reconciliation was: how the blacks and whites could live together after all the cruelty. Whites, or guilty blacks, were given a chance to get amnesty from punishment if they voluntarily confessed and showed remorse. There is still a video on YouTube of the cop who killed Biko who could not raise any remorse. He said Biko "bumped his head on a wall." I do not know what then became of the non-remorseful persons.

In my book *Reunion,* I suggested a way for groups to form committees to hear the protective parent tell her or his story with an eye to awarding a "chit to that person to go and collect the kid -- sort of a 70NAE rescue." I said "the passcode for imbuing good citizens with the right to issue chits was 'God is not mocked'."

Of course, groups can meet legally on the steps of any state's Parliament House to discuss issues. Will the bad guys send infiltrators to stoke violence? Well, they usually do.

Regarding grand juries in US, they were traditionally citizen led, but by a Rule (not a law), attorneys-general have claimed leadership of them. There is nothing to prevent you holding, in a fast-food restaurant if necessary, a make-believe Grand Jury. There is strength in numbers. Even three or four participants give ballast.

I suggest you carefully use the term "Make-Believe Grand Jury" to protect yourself. You could even produce subpoenas marked "Make-Believe subpoenas." The point is to take part in the law in the normal old way, and to feel good about it. Take care not to accuse someone of a crime in print, as you could be sued for defamation. (Deceased persons, however, cannot sue for defamation.) In the US, truth is an absolute defense if you get sued, so said SCOTUS in 1974 in *New York Times v Sullivan.*

29. Who Can Beautify Humanity? You, Me, Anyone Can

Lake Atitlan, Guatemala, Photo by Mark Harpur, 2018

My thinking on humanity owes much to two mentors -- Edward O Wilson in evolutionary biology and Philip Allott in...um...er... maybe there's no name for this field. Allott calls it philosophy. I'll call it Allotism. Here's an example from his book *Eutopia:*

9.12 "We can no longer surrender to false fatalism. and simply observe what the mind does ... as something which is inevitable and uncontrollable, a stage play in which we are not leading actors, let alone ... the author or the director. **The human mind contains the human future**. We need a special strength of mind, and rare optimism, to see that, in our past failures, there has always been the seed of new successes." [bolding added]

Well, that's a help after Part 4 on Kafka and Part 5 on Evils!

Please don't think Allott is airy-fairy. He's just way up. His 2016 book is his life's work, covering the sweep of history. Were you to ask him where our false fatalism comes from, he would look into neuroscience for the basis of human thinking and then at our creations some of which may be far off the track. Listen:

5.17 "We also now have plenty of evidence to suggest that the pursuit of total control of the minds of human beings ends in failure. People are remarkably resistant in the depth and integrity and energy of their minds, their self-defense against such an invading social force, seeking to make them think what they do not want to think, and feel what they do not want to feel." [Note: '5.17' means Chapter 5, paragraph 17 of his book.]

12.15: "We know immeasurably more about everything than all those who have gone before us ... and can access it at the touch of a button. Yet we do not feel correspondingly cleverer or wiser. Acquiring knowledge is no longer a crucial, and exciting, form of human experience. Knowledge has taken on the character of an inert thing... as an effect of its immensity and its availability."

I chose the title of my book "Society Is the Authority" under the influence of Allott. Oh, did I mention he is a law professor at Cambridge? Besides saying "Law is our anatomy and physiology," Allott says: "Law courts are an integral part of the ... self-creating of society and hence socially accountable for their decisions...."

10:24 "The central problem of law in human society is its relation to power. **All law is an exercise of power by human beings**, in its making, application and enforcement. As a consequence, there can be good law and bad law, good courts and bad courts.... Law can be a means of oppression and exploitation."

I'd like him to have a chat with the judge who ruled in *Argyle!*

10.29 "Two particular aspects have predominated in the installing of law in the deep-structure of society -- the problem of law in relation to *the totality of society*; the problem of the role of law in *the control of public power*." Both are crucial to the task of re-imagining and remaking the place of law now, and ... international law."

10:33 "**Rule of Law asserts the authority of law over all public power.**" 10.44 "**Law is an expression of a society's collective will to become what it chooses to be.**" 10.65 "It would take centuries of evolutionary constitutionalism **to find the basis for the authority of a society's law within the authority of that society as a whole....** [Often] the struggle led to civil war."

Dear Reader, are you getting the feel of this? Allott says, in caps, at end of his book: MAKERS OF THE NEW WORLD, UNITE!

End of Part Six: Future // **A ballad by Banjo Paterson**

There was movement at the station, for the word had got around that the colt from Old Regret had got away, and had joined the wild bush horses, he was worth a thousand pound, so all the cracks had gathered to the fray.

All the tried and noted riders from the stations far and wide had gathered at the homestead overnight, For the bushmen love hard riding where the wild bushes horses are, and the stockhorse snuffs the battle with delight.... And one was there, a stripling on a small and weedy beast something like a racehorse undersized....

Clancy said: He hails from Snowy River, up by Kosciusko's side, Where the hills are twice as steep and twice as rough, Where a horse's hoofs strike firelight from the flint stones every stride, The man that holds his own is good enough....

When they reached the mountain's summit, even Clancy took a pull, It well might make the boldest hold their breath, The wild hop scrub grew thickly, and the hidden ground was full Of wombat holes, and any slip was death. [The young one] sent the flint stones flying, but the pony kept his feet, He cleared the fallen timber in his stride, And the man from Snowy River never shifted in his seat It was grand to see that mountain horseman ride. Through the stringybarks and saplings down the hillside at a racing pace he went; And he never drew the bridle till he landed safe and sound, At the bottom of that terrible descent....

Then they lost him for a moment, where two mountain gullies met In the ranges, but a final glimpse reveals On a dim and distant hillside the wild horses racing yet, With the man from Snowy River at their heels. And he ran them single-handed till their sides were white with foam. He followed like a bloodhound on their track, Till they halted cowed and beaten, then he turned their heads for home, And alone and unassisted brought them back.

And down by Kosciusko, where the pine-clad ridges raise Their torn and rugged battlements on high, Where the air is clear as crystal, and the white stars fairly blaze At midnight in the cold and frosty sky, And where around The Overflow the reed beds sweep and sway To the breezes, and the rolling plains are wide, The man from Snowy River is a household word today, And the stockmen tell the story of his ride. (abridged) 1868

30. Conclusion: Roll Up Your Sleeves, and I Mean YOU

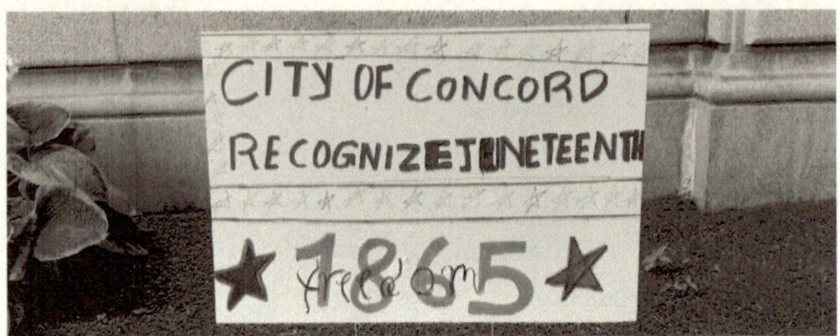

Local NH sign celebrates end of slavery. Well, the partial end of slavery...

It all comes down to what you are willing to do. We are all trapped in a disastrous situation at the moment. We are going only in one direction: towards a complete loss of human freedom and habitat and even loss of our human nature by manipulation of DNA.

I claim that much can be done by declouding people's minds and educating professionals, including lawyers, as to how we got where we are. The future could be brilliant.

So Much Woe in Our Civilized Western Societies

This book revealed a lot of human suffering, most of which seems unnecessary or even ludicrous. In order to protect a few people at the top, who are fixated on controlling the population, all sorts of crazy tricks have become common. "The Pridgeons of this world" are trying to pin down what's going on. Here are some of the things going on that got a mention in this book:

1. The Royal Commission's Final Report in 2017 showed 17,000 victims of **child sexual abuse** in Australia. These are 'historical' cases; current victims were not allowed to report, and the court-aided abuse did not get put on the table. How many thousands of these are there?

2. This book noted the **loss of livelihood** of doctors: Pridgeon, McBride, Trozzi, Luchkiw, and lawyers: Teffaha and Potkonyak. One cop, Denis Ryan, was forced out; he later got compo. One cop in Adelaide had to go into hiding for whistleblowing the drowning of George Duncan in the Torrens River. Plenty have been impoverished by legal expenses over false charges.

3. Some people got **wrongfully arrested**: Martin Bryant, Russell Pridgin, Patrick O'Dea, Cling Peaches, Wilfred Wong, Jahar Tsarnaev, Dieter Pfennig, James Earl Ray. Others were **falsely imprisoned**: Rosa Tsarnaeva at a motel, Barry Hart at Chelmsford Hospital, Karen Wetmore at Vermont State. How about all the children Family Court imprisons at home with abusive fathers?

4. Many **others were unfree** thanks to the outrageous MK-Ultra.

5. There is **harassment, stalking**, and break-ins of the homes of whistleblowers, plus unending trolling and slander of them. I think the trophy goes to Rachel Vaughan on that last one.

6. Mothers galore suffered the incredible **loss of contact** with their child, plus knowing that a psychologist was teaching the kid "not to lie" about having been abused. The mum lost her reputation as neighbors figured she was bad or was "mental." After several years of this she probably *would* go mental!

7. The ultimate punishment, **death**, is easily handed out by the Powers That Be. Tamerlan Tsarnaev and Ibragim Todashev were bumped off by the FBI, Troy Davis was wrongly executed, and Dr Rashid Buttar, an anti-vaxer, got poisoned. Phil Cam was killed so Karen Wetmore could be owned. These good people were called suiciders: Alyssa Peterson, Mark Minnie, Clare MacIntyre, Dr Jeff Bradstreet, and Georgia Senator Nancy Schaefer.

8. The following **died in hospital** and I think we know why: Freda Briggs, Sara Moore, John Magufuli, and Robert David Steele, not to mention William Combes regarding Kamloops.

9. Think how different the world would be today if **whistleblowers** had succeeded in getting things turned around. Had 9/11 critics been welcomed twenty years ago, we may not have fallen into the pit. Still, there remains a chance to wake up now.

10. Here are some current whistleblowers: Kevin Annett, Chris Steyn, Dee McLachlan, Corey Feldman, Fiona Barnett, Joachim Hagopian, Diane DeVere, Angela Power-Disney, Anneke Lucas, Kay Griggs, Cathi Morgan, and for that matter, Yours Truly.

Isn't Any of This Punishable by the Grace of Law?

Let's identify some crimes and torts discussed in this book. Remember: you need a government to prosecute a crime, but torts, i.e., lawsuits. are private law among members of society.

Crimes. These can all be found in statutes, not merely in common law: Murder, assault, stalking, harassment, theft, fraud, perjury, bribery, vacating records, tampering with a witness or juror, obstructing justice (in the US it's at 18 USC 1501ff). This includes denying due process to an accused, and covering up a crime -- coverup can make you an accessory after the fact. Gee. Racketeering is itself a crime, such as the human-trafficking racket.

Torts. The remedy for a tort is usually monetary damages. Torts include: Assault, trespass, defamation, harassment, theft, fraud, and wrongful death -- yes that's also a crime but the bereaved can sue. Don't forget malicious prosecution, for which Operation Noetic gets the trophy, and many species of fraud. Mums, please note 'IED' -- intentional infliction of emotional distress, a tort.

Roadblocks. This book pointed to ways in which the law fails to run its course. I mean, if you double-park you expect the law to run its course, don't you? So how come it goes into 'Duh' mode when Rachel tells SA Police where the bodies are buried?

I think the real roadblock is that the "Entitled" are running the show, but we can pause for a moment to rehearse lesser explanations. One roadblock is the brainfog around Australia's king. He, like his late mother, deserves respect as does every head of state. Yet Aussies look upon His/Her Majesty as a decoration on the "real" politics of Oz. Wrong, the **monarchy** is the real politics.

Also, the legal system in Oz is run by persons whom we don't know. Pridgeon's book drives this home. He was amazed to find that his medical license could be unlawfully suspended, and that members of the offending tribunal were **unaccountable**. By persisting, he got the decision corrected by NSW Supreme Court, but no punishment ensued for the liars at the Medical Council.

And who runs the **law schools**? My education at Adelaide gave me not a clue, not a hint, of the massive corruption within the judiciary. If judges won't apply the law, what is the use of our having a beautiful legal heritage? It would almost be better if the **judges dressed like thugs**, and shot on sight any upstarts in the gallery. (In the Cling Peaches trial, the judge ejected a pastor from the gallery. Well, I guess that's a start.)

Censorship. A significant trick in *King v Cling* is Judge Leanne Clare's use of suppression orders to keep people's brains from functioning. The cerebrum can't work until it registers sensory perception, right? Especially if you are a juror, you need to know who did what to whom. Who flung dung, as it were. Her Honor has also closed the court during part of the *Cling* trial. Shock city.

Media. Where is the media when Judge Wood hides the result of his Royal Commission? Doesn't a newspaper owner want to sell more copies and ads by publishing juicy material? Being a Murkin, I can't relate to 'D' notices and suppression orders. See SCOTUS' 1976 ruling in *Nebraska Press*: Prior restraint is a no-no. As in *NO*. Anyway, fie on the *Courier Mail* for utterly twisting O'Dea's story.

Workarounds. Sleeves rolled up, Everybody? Things you can legally take up were discussed in Chapter 28. Here's a recap:

Citizen's arrest, the law of outlawry, nullification of a bad law, act in self-defense (as in Don't lie there and take it), private prosecution, start a make-believe grand jury and issue make-believe subpoenas (Eagle Strong Voice Kevin Annett in the Republic of Kanata publishes arrest warrants, *and says he's made good with them.)*

I liked Karen **Brewer's** idea -- she asked citizens of Oz and NZ, all on a given day, to stand silently outside the Parliament House of their state, until the Governor came out and handed over the Senator Heffernan list of pedophiles. I mean why not? Karen stated that if they did not do so, they signaled their **resignation**. ("I don't want this job anymore.") As it happened, a truckers' protest, set for the very same hour, upended her event. Hmm.

I did not mention, but now propose, a re-opening of the Port Arthur massacre. **Justice** for **Martin Bryant** is urgent. I also propose a review of **Louise Bell's** death. We have a walkin', talk-in' eyewitness in Rachel Vaughan. What more can you ask? She proposes a reopening of every inquest ever handled by Coroner Mannock. Likewise, I suggest we examine all Judge Obradovic's NAE cases. And any case of Munchausen diagnosis of the mum.

The Court of Equity. I did not cover the important topic of Equity. In days of old, when knights were bold, the king had what Blackstone called "a court of equity in his bosom." You could go to His Maj for mercy, or for a constructive remedy. Yes, one can use the Maxims as a guide, not just statutes and precedents: the "great legal principles" can do wonders today. Our judiciary has hushed up the Court of Equity. So un-hush it! A fun aspect of it is that the baddy may be asked to disgorge his ill-gotten gains.

There's also a king's tradition of accepting corrections of mistakes that happened in a case. See my book *Fraud Upon the Court* on this.

The Authority of Society

So now we see, in all the above spectacle of holding law at bay, that there was never a need for us to be shy. The habit just developed. The notion that immunity prevails was a confusing element. Also, people have come to think of the cop or the judge as the source of authority. The real source is always the people.

Every culture constructs a picture of right and wrong. I suppose the basis of that is self-preservation. We like rules that are reasonably altruistic. We *want* there to be mutual obligations. Life is weird when each 'unit' acts in wild pursuit of self-advantage.

As shown in this book, the deviants do not seem to be mad egoists but act more like servants. They have their culture. Even if it's cuckoo (such as Satanism), it is a culture. They are obedient in the same way we good guys obey our culture. Nevertheless, it is peculiar how they go about theirs within a society that forbids their behavior. All our political leaders speak "normalese." You don't hear them boast "We've found a higher calling -- Satan is great!"

Start Small, but Start Immediately

Philip Allott, who knows his onions -- he was a UK diplomat -- says it's not too late for saving humanity, but it's "gettin' there." I recommend that everyone who was interested enough to read this book go out and start the countermove. I hope I have given you ammo to attack the baddies -- that is needed, and the public needs to see them fall from their perch. But we could also offer amnesty to baddies if they'll come out. They are so numerous!

I think it helps to see the major monsters as bluffing. You have to credit them for scaring us, but now we can call their bluff. Surely they bit off way more than they can chew. How many whistleblowers can they exterminate, or troll, or harass, or deceive?

As for the desire to harm children, and to make a veritable goal of it, there must be more to this sickness than we realize, but it should be realized that only a few at the top are pushing for it and most of their underlings may be glad to be relieved of the task.

It really comes down to you. Don't be lazy. Don't dread the embarrassment of looking silly. Go on, look silly; it's OK. At least set up a small meeting. Your local library has an obligation to let you use a lecture room. Will someone slash your tires? If they do, that's a good sign that you've become a threat to the overlords!

Now go back and re-read the penultimate chapter by Philip Allott. Just repeat after me, please: Society is the authority. Society is the authority. **Society is the authority**.

A Plea for MERCY for Dr Pridgeon

As you know, the first half of this book was about the situation in which Dr Russell Pridgeon found himself after an abusive dad harmed two girls and Russell tried to protect them. Looking back on the saga, it is apparent that the breakup of families is state policy (albeit hidden) in English-speaking countries. I think *that* is the larger plot, not the sexual urge known as pedophilia.

Let me now summarize the cruelty that Russell has been hit with. (It goes equally for O'Dea and the grandmother aliased as Cling Peaches, but I didn't have their details.) Australians should get Russell's back as this could happen to any of us:

1. Harassment. To name just a few things: His Commonwealth Bank account was fiddled with. He had to wear a leg tracker that required 2-hours of recharge. Bail rules curtailed any travel. The AFP took his computer. There were break-ins to his house (after which I'll bet Russell had to refrain from eating from any opened packages in the fridge). His dog died of poisoning -- classic.

2. Court$. Just like the sorrowing mums, he had to orient his life around dates of hearings, submission deadlines, and worry as to how much each episode would cost. After all of his assets disappeared into his defense, he ended up in penury.

3. This means he is now self-represented. Wouldn't you think some top-dog attorneys would want to work for him pro bono? Luckily he does have two brainy laypersons helping him whom he calls Angels. Otherwise, he'd have been incarcerated by now.

4. Loss of reputation must be fantastic for a doc who had taken doctorhood to be an honor. Upon writing to his colleagues in NSW, he got only one reply. And some patients cross the street rather than bump into Russell. (I see that as forgivable, given the media blast of Operation Noetic, portraying him as a creep.)

5. Part of the harassment, as such, were two bogus "Health Care Complaints" that caused him to have to face a tribunal. Judge Trench gave him no quarter but Court of Appeal did. In fact the *normalcy* of those Appeal judges is the sweetest thing in this book.

6. Pridgeon will tell you that all this is small beer, compared to his worry about the children, for whom no one showed interest. (For Grandma, it's worse; the stolen boy is her own flesh and blood.)

7. Magistrate Gett, formerly of the DPP, acted unlawfully in the case, refusing to hear about the kids' abuse which would render Russell in the clear, and not allowing police perjury to be noted. I think this may all be a way of conditioning us to "new reality."

8. The splitting off of the grandmother as a co-accused, caused disadvantage to Pridgeon and O'Dea in terms of witnesses. Hey, that must have been the intention. Really, who's in charge here? Doc must not be shown to have been trying to rescue abused kids, as that would cause Qld Crimes sec 286 to exonerate him.

9. Judge Clare's behavior is inexplicable. Her Honor has closed the court for part of Cling Peaches, and put suppression orders on other parts. She also ejected a pastor from the gallery. I know that would be reasonable if he yelled or threw shoes, but he did not. (Cling's case is now adjourned, due to jurors calling in sick.)

10. Long story short, the three "accused" Noetics must be experiencing anxiety and apprehension to the Nth degree. I hear that Patrick has war wounds that pain him all the time, now exasperated by this.

I am asking for mercy. I am asking people to recognize that, well, we don't have real law anymore. (Recall *Argyle*?) The men should be acquitted, or the charges dropped. Maybe the noble Seymours of South Africa will board a boat and come rescue the lot of us?

Make *The King v O'Dea & Pridgeon* go away! Bring back good Oz!

Photo of Russell (right) in happier times with Brother John, who is a doctor in Zimbabwe

HOLLIS (NEW-HAMPSHIRE) TOWN MEETING

At a legal Meeting of the Inhabitants of the Town of *Hollis*, in the Province of *New-Hampshire*, held on the 7th day of *November*, 1774, the following Resolves were unanimously passed, viz:

That we will at all times endeavour to defend our liberties and privileges, both civil and sacred, even at the risk of our lives and fortunes; and will not only disapprove of, but wholly despise all such persons as we have just and solid reason to think, even wish us in any measure deprived of the same.

That we do abhor, detest, and abominate all oppressive acts of persons in power, whether Magistrate or Officer, whereby the poor are distressed and robbed of their properties and will endeavour to treat them in such a manner as they justly deserve.

That we will at all times endeavour to assist the Civil Magistrate in the due execution of his office, and will always shew our dislike to all unlawful proceedings of unjust men, [who] outrageously trample underfoot the very law of liberty, and madly destroy that jewel which is so exceeding precious....

****

To the Honorable Committee of Safety for Hillsborough, NH: Gentlemen, Your congratulatory address on my appointment to Brigadier-General demands my thanks. Your approbation of my conduct while at the bar, acting in defense of an injured people against the arbitrary Tools of Government gives me highest satisfaction. Your most obedient servant, John Sullivan, 1775

****

Blank form: I, _____, do solemnly swear that I will do my duty, that I will to the utmost of my power Disclose and make Known to some officer or Magistrate all plots & conspiracies which may come to my knowledge against this state or the United States and that I will not give aid or advice or any Intelegence to any person acing under the Authority of the said King.
-- from *Towns Against Tyranny*, ed by William Gardner, 1976

AFTERWORD: Lexmen and Association Papers

Dear Young People,

We oldsters won't be around much longer. We are, or were, the keepers of the marvelous achievements of centuries. We're dying for you to pick up on this. Trust me, the way things are today is quite odd. Naturally you take it as normal -- it's in the landscape. But I'm pretty sure it was *designed* to rob us of our natural joys.

My best guess is that it's all in the hands of a very few designers at the top. More than a hundred years of their work is recorded. They had to keep thinking of better and better ways to preclude any challenge to their wealth and social advantage. You have heard of "the One Percent"? Do you think it's wise that we let 1% of mankind own more than what the majority own, all up?

In this book I revealed -- to my own surprise -- that Australia has so turned normalcy upside down that people obey an authority whose daily job (cops, judges, legislators) is actually to create hurt and harm. Clearly we need to rename them, as their very name, "law enforcement," wrongly stirs a moral impulse.

I can't ask you to be rebels, as that would incur the wrath of the many citizens who automatically assume that our law enforcers are moral and that opposing them is immoral. Rather, I now propose that you give yourself the name "lexmen." Yes, you should oppose any wrong-doing "law enforcers" but not as rebels, rather as the correct or righteous law enforcers. I grabbed the word *lex* which is Latin for law. Come up with a better term if you wish. The idea is that you are protecting real, good law.

We don't operate in the environment of the 18th century New Hampshire men quoted above. I don't see how we can strike out militarily against our overlords. I suggest that we sort out who is with us and who is against. Folks in Hillsborough NH came up with the idea of **Association Papers**. They worried that some of their neighbors preferred to side with the Brits. So they asked everyone to sign under oath as to their chosen loyalty. Those who chose loyalty to King George III were to be disarmed.

You can make up the wording for today's Association Paper. It will be voluntary in that we have no power to disarm the bad guys. I suggest you make the Association Paper friendly so that anyone would like to sign. Something along the lines of "I __ do solemnly swear that I am not engaged in any opposition to the US Constitution. I will not act against the rights of the people."

But if you are approaching an official, the message could contain an additional point as to his/her accountability. "I ___ do swear that I take orders only from proper officials. I do not belong to any secret society or other group that commands my loyalty or adherence." You'd perhaps mention that false oaths are perjury.

In my salad days, say the 1960s, we were not yet economically trapped. But today the whole world is trapped in a unified economy. There is nowhere to run, nowhere to hide. Possibly this is making people feel that they have lost any sense of self-help.

This economic entrapment is scheduled to include removal of all cash. cash. We will each be rated on a social credit score as to our worthiness to spend "points" or whatever you call it, from our bank account. Just imagine a few (at the top) thinking they have the right to micro-manage the life of every citizen.

And what is the criterion that they will apply to determine your "worthiness"? It directly reflects their own major need, which is to make sure we don't do anything to harm their position. Really this means they live in fear -- but possibly they do not consciously know it. Look at the incredible effort they put into this major scheme of controlling the masses. And just think of the price paid for it, in our suffering.

Supposedly these jerks are also sponsoring the science of transhumanism to make us less like we are today, that is, less human. I think this is largely a result of science having found the means to alter the genetic code. It's rare, isn't it, for anyone with the capacity to do such-and-such, to hold back and not do it.

There are also plans for massive destruction via war. George Orwell was already aware, in 1949, when he wrote *1984*, that the cause of war was strictly cynical -- to protect the life of the 1%.

Much of my work has consisted of finding fault with the justice system, including the courts. I see an uninterrupted pattern of the prosecutors and judges protecting from punishment anyone who is doing terrible things to us. If citizens come soon to the realization of this, they will be better able to resist it. The tradition of worship of anyone in a judicial robe is a major problem. Many judges are acting criminally, so lets' say so.

Look at how easily we all accept that there are hidden rulers. Excuse me, there should be no hidden rulers. If they want to rule us, let them show their wares. Let's chat with them, draft some contracts with them. What? They won't do that? Then off with their heads.

Undoubtedly, we cannot avoid or even postpone this task. We cannot decline to act. Their recent incursions are new and are terrific. The "authorities" in Canberra have recently used radiation weapons on peaceful protestors. Many folks got skin burns and said they are nauseated and headachy.

This is a direct, unprovoked, unjustified, unlawful physical attack. We can't let it ride. Radiation weapons can be directed at whole cities, whole countries. They can put your brain out of commission. And once your brain is out of commission, that's the end of your being able to get the upper hand.

Get the upper hand? Is that possible? Of course it's possible. Granted, the decision makers have huge staffs working for them. Three reasons why those staffs don't "turn state's witness" -- or, should I say, turn people's witness, are: 1. They fear retaliation. (Who wouldn't?) 2. They are mind controlled and are not in contact with their own will. (I think that may be a far greater issue than we have imagined.) and 3. They are willing to contact us but don't know which of us is OK.

Set up a lexmen office. Or call it a poetry office and read the occasional poem. Or a rubbish-cleanup seminar. Invite people to show up and bitch. Keep it fun. What if you try and you fail? At least you will have tried! Give interested persons your email address. Here's mine: MaxwellMaryLLB@gmail.com. Love, MM

BIBLIOGRAPHY

About the Author

Mary Maxwell graduated from Emmanuel College, Boston in 1969 with a BA, and got an MLA from Johns Hopkins in 1979. She married into Australia in 1980 and from 1988 to 1993 she and her spouse lived in the United Arab Emirates. Mary has a PhD in Politics and a law degree from University of Adelaide.

Her first four books were published by university presses while she was still a 'presentable' person; the next three were published by Trine Day when she was a quiet dissident. But since 2015 she has had to self-publish -- fancy that, in the Land of the Free Press! Mary has produced five plays at the Adelaide Fringe Festival, one of them being a moot court trial for the never-tried Martin Bryant. She likes to file useful lawsuits against the US government.

Acknowledgements

Special thanks for 'morale' during the gestation of this book, to: Rob, Eileen, Craig, Jo, Graeme, the K's, Shelley, Kosmos, Simon, Pie, Prema, and Costica. *Danke* to Don Jeffries for broadcasting my *Cling Peaches* lecture. 'Onya' to the inestimable survivors, and a ton of empathy to the parents whom our society has devastated.

INDEX

www.ingramcontent.com/pod-product-compliance
Lightning Source LLC
LaVergne TN
LVHW091316150826
845673LV00006B/1672
9798891212657